Best Leadership Practices for High-Poverty Schools

Linda L. Lyman
Christine J. Villani

ScarecrowEducation
Lanham, Maryland • Toronto • Oxford
2004

Published in the United States of America
by Scarecrow Press, Inc.
An imprint of The Rowman & Littlefield Publishing Group, Inc.
4501 Forbes Boulevard, Suite 200, Lanham, Maryland 20706
www.scarecroweducation.com

PO Box 317
Oxford
OX2 9RU, UK

Photographs in chapter 2 by Linda Lyman
Photographs in chapter 3 by Christine Villani

British Library Cataloguing in Publication Information Available

Library of Congress Cataloging-in-Publication Data

Lyman, Linda L.
  Best leadership practices for high-poverty schools / Linda L. Lyman,
Christine J. Villani.
       p. cm.
  Includes bibliographical references and index.
  ISBN 1-57886-079-2 (pbk. : alk. paper)
  1. Poor children—Education—United States. 2. Educational
leadership—United States. 3. Elementary school principals—United
States—Case studies. I. Villani, Christine J. II. Title.
LC4091 .L96 2004
371.826'942–dc22   2003022291

Manufactured in the United States of America.

With love and gratitude, we dedicate this book to our families.

My husband, Dave Weiman,
and children
Steve Gale and Beth Bear,
Elaine Gale,
David and Kristine Gale,
and two grandsons,
Jack Gale and Charlie Gale

L.L.L.

My husband, Kevin McGinley,
and son, Matthew Villani

C.J.V.

Contents

Tables and Photographs

Tables

Photographs

Acknowledgments

We gratefully acknowledge the help and support of all the named and unnamed persons who contributed to this book, including the many other scholars whose research about high-poverty schools and social justice leadership has informed and enlightened us. The book would not have been written if ScarecrowEducation managing editor Cindy Tursman had not attended our AERA presentation in Seattle in 2001 and invited us to submit a book proposal about leadership in high-poverty schools. We are grateful for her encouragement and confidence in our work.

L.L.L. and C.J.V.

I am particularly grateful to Aurthur Perkins for sharing time, energy, and the wisdom acquired from her many years of experience as a teacher and principal in a high-poverty school. Spending time with her, the faculty and staff, and the children at Harrison Primary School has enriched my understanding and life in profound ways. I appreciate College of Education dean Dianne Ashby, department chair Patricia Klass, and my colleagues in the Department of Educational Administration and Foundations at Illinois State University who supported my work on this project in every way. Thanks also to doctoral student and graduate assistant Stefanie McAllister, who provided invaluable research assistance and transcribed the interview tapes. Finally, Dave Weiman offered a husband's love and support, keeping our household functioning when I became totally absorbed with the book. Moreover, his encouraging enthusiasm for my work is an intangible treasure I value beyond all measure.

L.L.L.

I am grateful to Carmen Perez-Dickson for her generosity of time and her willingness to impart her wisdom from years of experience as a principal in an urban city. I am also grateful to her faculty, staff, and parents who were welcoming and generous with their time and with their willingness to share their stories. Thanks are also owed to the College of Education at Southern Connecticut State University, my colleagues, and my students who listened intently to my beliefs and ideas. Finally, to my wonderful son, Matthew, and my loving husband, Kevin, for their support, and to my "sister," Camille Brady, for many hours of coffee. She was a great sounding board.

C.J.V.

Chapter One

Poverty and School Leadership

School leaders, particularly in urban areas, find large percentages of their students and families living in poverty. In rural areas, the number of students and families living in poverty continues to increase as well. A book on best leadership practices for high-poverty schools is timely, as the achievement gap for poor and minority students continues to grow. According to Scherer (2002–2003):

> The color line that W. E. B. Du Bois so insightfully identified as the 20th century's biggest problem has become an achievement gap in the 21st. *The gap now measures four years long* [italics added]. By the end of high school, African American and Latino students have skills in both reading and mathematics that are virtually identical to those of white students at the end of middle school. . . . The gap has grown worse in the past ten years. (5)

Creating successful environments for learning in high-poverty schools involves providing support for families as well as care and challenge for students. In too many high-poverty schools, learning needs of students and their families are not being met. Schools need informed, compassionate, and committed leaders who have the knowledge, skills, and attitudes to create successful learning environments. We know these schools exist and that within each are dedicated principals, teachers, and staff members who understand the complexities of poverty and view the students as filled with promise.

The 2002 No Child Left Behind legislation is an attempt to improve schools that are failing to teach all students well. The logic of the law would change the conditions of education for children in failing schools by mandating accountability for learning. On a rhetorical level, the law seems an attempt to change widespread complacency about the large numbers of poor and minority children who do not meet state standards for learning at acceptable levels. Required achievement test scores must rise or schools will face the consequences. But what matters most in any reform, particularly in changing the learning environments of high-poverty schools, cannot be mandated (Fullan 1993). Changing the learning environments of low-performing, high-poverty schools requires changing the beliefs and attitudes of educators.

Writing about attitudes affecting school reform, particularly reforms addressing schools for children living in poverty, Siegel quotes Pedro Noguera, a researcher and sociologist who studies urban education: "Across the political spectrum and ingrained throughout very different school systems, says Noguera, is a persuasive and passive acceptance of the 'fact' that students from low-income backgrounds cannot achieve at the levels of students from privileged backgrounds" (2002, 51). Noguera points out that most school reform fails to use a holistic approach that takes into account the culture of the school and the relationships within the school. He understands learning failures to be failures of connection between schools and their students, stating that educators need to stop viewing the problem of low achievement as within the student and begin "considering what adults can do to engage kids more in their educational experiences" (Siegel, 52).

Other scholars have also identified low expectations as being at the root of low achievement in high-poverty schools. For example, Delpit faults teacher preparation: "Teacher education usually focuses on research that links failure and socioeconomic status, failure and cultural difference, and failure and single-parent households. It is hard to believe that these children can possibly be successful after their teachers have been so thoroughly exposed to so much negative indoctrination" (1995, 172). She identifies teacher education programs as "a primary source of stereotyping" (172). Delpit's view is that deficit assumptions lead teachers who have no knowledge of the students' lives outside of the classroom to teach less to students culturally different from themselves. The teachers see deficits rather than strengths. "Because teachers do not want to tax what they believe to be these students' lower abilities, they end up teaching less when, in actuality, these students need *more* of what school has to offer" (173). In advocating for culturally responsive teaching practices, Gay (2000) also insists that low achievement is a symptom of a problem for which the "why" continues to be unanswered because educators keep looking within the students for explanations.

Hafer simply views educators as unaware prisoners of an outmoded paradigm. "We view everything from within a set of boundaries that defines our behavior. Education's paradigm is omnipresent. Everyone, especially most educators, views schooling within boundaries, according to rules set hundreds of years ago. . . . An axiom of a paradigm is that once inside you cannot feel its embrace" (2000, 7–8). He argues that believing all children can learn is essential for bringing about change and reforming education. The belief that all children can learn, although often invoked, is a belief currently outside the paradigm, he contends. Stating that "equality in educational performance has always been outside the paradigm," Hafer eloquently poses the key question: "This issue is the crux, the most important confronting America and public education. Can we break out of the paradigm and come to believe that we can educate every student at a high level, except those with physiological disabilities that prevent learning?" (45).

We believe that leadership from the heart of a moral commitment is required to educate every student at a high level and to change deeply ingrained beliefs and attitudes about poverty, including belief in the inevitability of low achievement in high-poverty schools. Such transformative leadership anchors best practices in values of social justice (Shields 2003). Describing transformative cross-cultural leaders as authentic and purposeful, Shields uses these words:

> Leaders who are authentic—consistent in words and actions, committed to a moral cause, and willing to take a stand—may differ widely in their goals, personality traits, or leadership styles, yet they can all be successful leaders. They are transformative, working for change wherever they find inequity. They are cross-cultural, working with people from many different cultural groups in order to enhance equity for all. (28–29)

Fullan (2003) writes about system transformation as the ultimate goal of reform efforts, but still offers insights about building-level leadership. He explains how a leader changes the context by being able "to introduce new elements into the situation that are bound to influence behavior for the better" (1). Although the socioeconomic profile of a school cannot be changed, the context can, he argues. Changing the context in a school requires creating a supportive community in which new behaviors and beliefs can be developed and nurtured. Fullan writes, "We are beginning to obtain a glimpse of the new moral imperative of school leadership. At the school level . . . the moral imperative of the principal involves leading deep cultural change that mobilizes the passion and commitment of teachers, parents, and others to improve the learning of all students, including closing the achievement gap" (41). As principals develop the leadership of others in the school community, collective inquiry and relational trust make change of this magnitude possible (Bryk and Schneider 2002). For a principal, Fullan explains, "What I am saying is that the driver should be moral purpose and that all other capacities (e.g., knowledge of the change process, building professional learning communities) should be in the service of moral purpose" (2003, 30). In other words, Fullan contends and we agree that the leader's beliefs rather than particular leadership strategies are of primary importance in any process of changing and improving a school.

PURPOSE OF THIS BOOK

Stereotypes about the poor and widespread misconceptions about poverty have influenced educators and permeate our society. The beliefs and attitudes of educators about poverty may be a major factor in the failure of high-poverty schools to create engaging, achievement-centered, learning environments for students. Beliefs of many educators about causes of poverty and why children living in poverty fail to achieve reflect *deficit thinking* about the children and their families. Particularly when the children come from racial and ethnic minority groups, too many educators see only children with problems and limited potential instead of children of promise. Deficit thinking colors their perceptions. According to Valencia (1997), "This brilliant two-word phrase [deficit thinking] was invented by a small cadre of scholars in the early 1960s who launched an assault on the orthodoxy that asserted the poor and people of color caused their own social, economic, and educational problems" (x). He asserts, "Of the various conceptual frameworks that have been advanced to explain school failure among low-income minority groups, the deficit thinking theory has held the longest currency among scholars, educators, and policymakers" (xi). Those with this view tend to hold the educational system and its practices blameless in the failures of students to learn.

Deficit thinking has taken many forms and is deeply embedded in an American culture that sees poverty as having largely individualistic rather than systemic or structural causes. A contemporary variation of deficit thinking is the labeling of children from low-income families as "at risk." Educational leaders must reexamine and become aware of their own belief systems about poverty. The complexity of poverty must be understood. If caught in deficit thinking themselves, leaders cannot hope to productively move faculty and staff in a positive direction—toward high expectations, effective teaching practices, and a firm belief that all children can learn.

Over four years ago, we began studying the issues of poverty and educational leadership. Through learning activities in leadership preparation classes in our own universities, we documented changes in students' beliefs and attitudes about poverty. We investigated educational leadership programs throughout the nation, surveyed and interviewed educators and educational leaders, observed in various schools in high-poverty areas, and studied the work of other scholars. Through this immersion in the issues of poverty and school leadership, we came to understand that beliefs and attitudes are at the heart of best leadership practices in high-poverty schools. The purpose of our book is to share this understanding and what we have learned about the issues of poverty and school leadership. Our work has focused on elementary schools, the level where examples of successful high-poverty schools have been most plentiful. We center the presentation of what we have learned on case studies of two actual leaders from high-performing, high-poverty elementary schools. These leaders understand the complexities of poverty and have clearly rejected all forms of deficit thinking about the children and families served by their schools. Each has had a transformative influence on a school community. Each leads a school committed to academic, personal, and social development. Each is an exemplar of best leadership practices for high-poverty schools. Although we have focused on elementary principals, we believe these case studies hold implications for middle and high school principals as well.

UNDERSTANDING THE COMPLEXITIES OF POVERTY

Poverty is a worldwide issue yet most of us know very little about the facets of poverty or the multiple frustrations of living in poverty. Millions of people are hungry, have no place to live, and no medical care, even though they may be working full time. From the perspective of one social critic, "As a nation we have become passive, refusing to act responsibly toward the more than thirty-eight million citizens who live in poverty here and the working masses who labor long and hard but still have difficulty making ends meet. The rich are getting richer. And the poor are falling by the wayside. At times it seems no one cares" (hooks 2000, 1).

Instead, as a country, we have become obsessed with getting people off welfare. Over the years, welfare has come to include a variety of programs that provide support for food, medical care, housing, job training, and education. Because many perceive the poor to be undeserving, the conversation in America focuses on *welfare* rather than on *poverty*. The attention is on who should receive welfare, who should provide it, and who should pay for it. Discussions surround what to do about welfare instead of what we could do to diagnose and address the basic causes of poverty (Chamberlin 2001).

Complacency was fostered as welfare rolls shrank and estimates of the numbers of children living in poverty appeared to be falling. According to official figures, the total number of children living below the poverty line fell from 12.1 million in 1998 to 11.6 million, or one in six children, in 2000. This was the lowest number in twenty years, a decrease attributed to the high-performing economy. The decline halted in 2001, however, when 11.7 million children were reported to be living in poverty (Children's Defense Fund 2002). During this same general time period, child poverty rose in full-time working families. "The number of poor children who live in families with a full-time year-round worker rose to 4.1 million in 2000, up from 3.8 million in 1999—a rise of 326,000 children—according to an analysis of Census Bureau data by the Children's Defense Fund" (Children's Defense Fund 2003). Approximately 16 percent of America's children (almost 12 million) live below the federal poverty line, which was $14,255 for a family of three in 2001 (Lu 2003).

Even these numbers do not convey the true extent of poverty. In the 1950s, the poverty line was established as a baseline for determining who was entitled to welfare programs. These programs became our means for eradicating poverty. "In the United States, during the War on Poverty in the mid-1960s, the poverty standard was calculated on the Orshansky Index, which assumed that low-income families spent roughly a third of their income on food" (Polakow 1993, 44). The poverty line is acknowledged by officials inside the government and others from concerned groups to be too low. We concur. "In the United States, the official framing of the poverty line minimizes the reality of poverty experienced by millions of children in families struggling to provide the necessities of survival, whether they are officially poor or not, and thereby provides an example of policy serving other political and economic priorities than the well-being of America's children" (Lyman and Villani 2002, 249). In fact, according to the National Center for Children in Poverty (Lu 2003), 38 percent of American children (27 million children) live in low-income families. Appallingly, 7 percent, or 5 million children, live in extreme poverty with incomes below half (or $7,127 for a family of three in 2001) of the official poverty line (Lu 2003).

Types of Poverty

Many in the general public assume the term *poor person* refers to someone who, because of his or her own failures, lacks money and other resources. Therefore, for years, society has focused its concern for the poor on how to change their behaviors as well as meet at some level their needs for food, housing, and employment. Poverty is also about economics, about what the continuing existence of the poor does for the society. The employed or working poor are caught in a systemic poverty that is perpetuated by the middle- and upper-class lifestyles that require keeping a percentage of individuals in low-paying, low-status jobs. This system of poverty is fostered by capitalism, cultural values, and attitudes about poverty within American society (Chamberlin 2001).

Welfare poor rather than *working poor* is what most people think of when they hear the term *poverty*. Welfare poor is tied to the poverty line established in the 1950s. The poverty line determines who is officially poor and therefore eligible for assistance programs. A family is considered poor only when their net income falls below a specific level, usually without regard for other objective evidence of poverty such as lack of indoor heating, indoor plumbing, medical care, transportation, or nutritional meals (Biddle 2001).

Tied to concepts of welfare and working poor are both generational and situational poverty, as well as urban and rural poverty. They are all intertwined. Whereas students of welfare and working poverty look at the economic categories of the poor, those concerned with generational and situational poverty examine the characteristics, family patterns, and situations that may place a person in poverty. Urban and rural poverty can originate simply from the geographical location of people's lives. In spite of this complexity, the common stereotype is that a poor person is minority, female, and lives in an urban area. Additionally, the typical beliefs and attitudes are that poor people are lazy, genetically deficient, and lack the appropriate skills and knowledge to live any better. Furthermore, the failure to educate poor children is seen as a cultural failure of the parents to provide appropriate support within their families (Biddle 2001).

Each of these variants of poverty will be explored further to reframe thinking about causes of poverty, and to establish that other reasons for poverty exist than race and gender. For example, Chamberlin (2001) lists reasons for being poor that interact with the different types of poverty. These reasons include:

- *Addiction*. An individual who is chemically dependent risks health, legal problems, and job loss, any of which can lead to poverty.
- *Catastrophic Illness*. A major illness such as cancer can lead to astronomical costs that place a person in poverty. Low-income families are in particular jeopardy because they generally lack medical coverage.
- *Disaster*. Poverty can occur due to floods, tornadoes, or simply being a victim of crime.
- *Disability*. Individuals who are disabled by physical or mental handicaps can often work but may experience poverty when unable to find a job.
- *Unemployment*. Persons over forty face the potential of losing their jobs and being replaced by younger people. Some give up after lengthy attempts to find a job. Many people find themselves unemployed and in poverty when businesses or factories close.
- *Elderly*. The elderly in our society are often the unknown and unseen poor. Some live only on Social Security; some have no Social Security. Many have to make hard choices such as whether to buy food or medication because they cannot afford both.

- *Mental Illness*. Mental illness is just like any other illness, can happen to anyone, and can be temporary. However, the stigma associated with it may cause persons to become caught in a cycle of poverty.
- *Employed at Minimum Wage*. These are the working poor whose salaries are inadequate to cover the necessities of life.
- *Cycles of Poverty*. This term describes poverty that appears to be passed on in a family system as generation after generation live on welfare or otherwise struggle to make ends meet.

Working Poor and Welfare Poor

Numbers of families receiving welfare do not tell the whole story of poverty in the United States. Close to two-thirds of the children living in poverty have at least one parent working. Writer Barbara Ehrenreich (2001a) experienced working poverty when she attempted as an experiment to support herself over a period of three months in three cities on entry-level wages. In a series of jobs, Ehrenreich worked as a waitress, a maid with a housecleaning service, hotel housekeeper, nursing home aide, and a Wal-Mart clerk. She could not make ends meet with just one job on the average salary of $7.00 an hour. The salary did not enable her to meet bare-bones expenses such as food, gas, and especially rent. Some people she worked with coped by devising various strategies such as sharing expenses with another breadwinner or working two jobs. Generally, one job with an eight-hour shift was followed by another job with a six-hour shift. Many passed up company health insurance because they could not afford the employee contribution. Some of the people she worked with were homeless, although those who had a car to live in did not consider themselves homeless. People often skipped meals, as did their family members, including children. Sometimes meals consisted of a bag of Doritos or potato chips. Ehrenreich concluded the following about the situation of the working poor: "These experiences are not part of a sustainable lifestyle, even a lifestyle of chronic deprivation and relentless low-level punishment. They are, by almost any standard of subsistence, emergency situations. And that is how we should see the poverty of so many millions of low-wage Americans—as a state of emergency" (2001a, 214).

Welfare reform has been declared a success, with over 60 percent of former recipients making their own way in the job market and the official poverty rate declining (Ehrenreich 2001b). However, looking closely, the picture is not pleasant. The Economic Policy Institute released a report demonstrating that 29 percent of families in the United States with young children do not earn enough income to live at an acceptable level of comfort or security (Boushey, Brocht, Gunderson, and Bernstein 2001). The EPI researchers reached this conclusion by calculating the very basic budget a family needs. This basic budget includes housing, clothing, food, health insurance, transportation, utilities, and child care. They discovered that the income of one-third of American families couldn't meet these basic needs. The EPI report verifies that the government still calculates poverty in an archaic fashion by taking the minimal cost of food for a family of a given size and multiplying it by three. Using this method, the U.S. government places the poverty line at an income of $17,463 for a family of four. No consideration is given to the rising cost of rent, medical insurance, medical care, and child care. Government leaders in the United States still conceive poverty to be a result of unemployment; therefore, the assumption that moving the poor from welfare into the workforce solves the problem. The EPI report demonstrates that poverty is not just a lack of work but a complex reality resulting from a constellation of conditions.

August 2001 marked the fifth anniversary of the landmark federal welfare reform law. The 1996 Personal Responsibility and Work Opportunity Reconcilation Act was enacted at a time when the economy of the United States was booming. This booming economy of the 1990s, however, did not extend to the more than 32 million people in America who cannot buy food, clothing, shelter, or health care without assistance (Weinberg 2001). People who live in poor communities live in cities, towns, and rural areas that are in various states of economic decay with no help in sight. The people who live in these communities cannot meet the basic needs of life. According to a government report (U.S. Census Bureau 2001), 17 percent of America's children and 21 percent of two-parent families did not receive the benefits of the booming economy of the 1990s. Large numbers of families are still living in poverty and the physical, mental, and social development of their children may be severely affected if this condition continues.

Generational and Situational Poverty

Two other forms of poverty are generational and situational poverty. According to Payne (1998), generational poverty refers to having been in poverty for at least two generations and situational poverty refers to a lack of resources due to a particular event. People in situational poverty include individuals who have chemical addictions, suffer a catastrophic illness that uses the majority of their financial resources, become disabled due to work-related or illness-related events, suffer a disaster such as the loss of a home, suffer a divorce, or suffer a temporary mental illness. In addition, the elderly are a group of people who fit under the classification of situational poverty when they have only Social Security income on which to live. Some without Social Security must begin to rely on public assistance (Chamberlin 2001). Payne states that generational poverty has "its own culture, hidden rules, and belief systems" (1998, 64). People in situational poverty bring resources with them that allow them to cope, while those in generational poverty typically do not. She differentiates between generational and situational poverty in terms of attitudes, saying that one of the major attitudes of those in generational poverty is that society owes them a living while those in situational poverty have pride and generally refuse assistance. Other differences occur in family patterns, language skills, and ability to establish support systems.

According to Payne (1998), people who live in generational poverty have unique family patterns that differ from those in situational poverty. Those in situational poverty have more typical family patterns that can be traced: marriage and divorces are documented, as are maternal and paternal identities as they relate to children. People in generational poverty tend to have scattered family patterns with multiple overlaps and common-law marriages. Siblings do not necessarily have the same parents. The only common denominator is that these are mother-centered family organizations.

People who live in generational poverty are at a disadvantage in terms of language skills, according to Payne (1998). Explaining communication patterns, Payne advances concepts from the work of Joos in the 1960s as part of his research on language and cultural diversity. Joos developed the idea that every language has five registers or levels: frozen, formal, consultative, casual, and intimate. Formal language is defined as the language of Standard English with correct syntax and vocabulary. Payne argues that people who are in generational poverty simply do not use formal language, complicating their ability to obtain jobs and their children's ability to do well in school. In contrast, people in situational poverty have a solid formal language base that aids in their ability to help themselves get out of temporary states of poverty. Stout (1996) discusses language as one of those invisible walls that keep minority and low-income persons from entering the ranks of the middle class. Language acts as an invisible wall that causes people to be viewed as less intelligent or inarticulate. Stout explains, "As anyone who has traveled in a foreign country knows, when you are speaking in a language outside your own, it is much harder to communicate. It is a barrier to feeling powerful" (123). Language patterns can contribute to a sense of powerlessness.

Tied to language is the ability to establish support systems (Payne 1998). Lack of skills with formal language makes it difficult for those in generational poverty to obtain the necessary resources they need to assist themselves. They may experience difficulties communicating with those who administer the systems of support. People in situational poverty have stronger coping strategies and the ability to problem solve and seek the resources that they need. Additionally, emotional resources are more often lacking for people in generational poverty than those in situational poverty. Because people in generational poverty live within dysfunctional systems where their needs cannot be met, developing resources to lift themselves out of poverty is challenging. They lack the emotional support of a system in which individuals have rules, roles, and relationships.

Payne (1998) states that more and more children are bringing to school a culture of poverty that is generational. Those in situational poverty could move into generational poverty if the resources they need become unavailable to them over time. Payne believes that the key to getting out of generational poverty is education. She asserts that individuals leave poverty for one of four reasons: a goal or vision, a painful situation, someone sponsors them, or a talent or ability gives them an opportunity. She argues that being in poverty is not about intelligence or ability, that most people in generational poverty just do not know that they have a choice, and that there is another way.

Urban and Rural Poverty

One hears and reads about the peril of America's poor, and specifically of America's poor children. In every state in the nation, children are more likely than adults to be poor (Nadel and Sagawa 2002). When people think of poor children, the immediate thought is urban poor. However, the plight of children who live in poverty extends beyond urban areas. Rural America is home to 2.5 million poor children. Children who live in rural areas often do not have access to medical care, electricity, uncontaminated water, transportation, or proper educational facilities (Cottle 2001). In a report issued by the Save the Children Foundation (Nadel and Sagawa 2002), *America's Forgotten Children: Child Poverty in Rural America*, several key findings from recent research are listed:

- Rural America is home to 2.5 million children locked in deep poverty.
- Rural poverty is highly concentrated in six regions of the country (Central Appalachia, the Deep South, the Rio Grande border, the Southwest, the Central Valley of California, and the American Indian Reservations in the Northern Plains).
- Child poverty is greater in rural America than in urban areas. Of 200 counties persistently poor, 195 are rural, with child poverty rates often exceeding 35 percent.
- Rural poverty has begun to mirror urban poverty in the past decade.

Rural poverty differs from urban poverty in that rural poverty exists in very isolated communities where there are few human and economic resources. Because of the isolation, rural poor children actually have greater disadvantages than urban children. They do not receive the same level of health care, many communities are dumping grounds for toxic waste and pollutants, and most children lack the basic necessities made possible by electricity. Phones and computers are virtually nonexistent. According to Nadel and Sagawa, the lack of industry or potential economic growth in these areas exacerbates the situation.

Education in rural America may be substandard. Less money per student is spent on education in rural America than anywhere else. In 1999, 40 percent of U.S. public schools were in rural small towns that enrolled 26 percent of public school students. These rural towns only received 23 percent of federal education dollars. Rural students fall behind their urban and suburban peers in high school and only 16 percent of rural children obtain college degrees (Nadel and Sagawa 2002). Rural children have very few, if any, options for after-school programs. Rural areas are less likely to have extended after-school programs, rarely have community centers or other safe places for children, and lack opportunities for sports and after-school activities. Close to 40 percent of the rural population have no access to public transportation and more than 57 percent do not own cars (Nadel and Sagawa 2002).

Finally, the poor in rural American are severely underserved by health care (Nadel and Sagawa 2002). The shortage of doctors, dentists, and other health care specialists is overwhelming, affecting approximately 68 percent of rural areas. More than 50 percent of rural children do not have health insurance and the death rates for children and young adults are highest in rural areas. Suicide rates are higher among rural children and substance abuse is significantly higher in rural areas than urban areas. According to a recent report (National Center on Addiction and Substance Abuse 2001), eighth graders in rural areas were using cocaine, taking amphetamines, and smoking marijuana at close to double the rates of their urban counterparts. Adolescents in tenth through twelfth grades used drugs and alcohol and were involved in drug trafficking at a rate two times higher than their urban peers.

Governmental programs have focused their energies and resources on poor urban children. Urban poverty, the phenomenon most people refer to when discussing poverty, presents contrasts, including more options for supportive social services and more opportunity for discouragement among the poor. Urban poverty is often concentrated in what are called ghetto neighborhoods within major American cities. Yet because these neighborhoods are close to downtown offices populated with affluent Americans, most urban poor daily confront America's abundance. Many enter an endless cycle of trying to obtain what their surrounding neighbors have. Yet the disappearance and removal of jobs to the suburbs, inappropriate tax funding structures, and lack of local government support have led to dilapidated housing in their neighborhoods, low incomes, minimal educational opportunities (in comparison to their suburban neighbors), and mediocre health care. These failed structures and supports contribute to cycles of crime, violence, and drug use within urban communities (Biddle 2001).

Educationally, urban children could be said to fare somewhat better than their rural counterparts. According to the U.S. Department of Education, approximately $2,000 more per student is spent on children living in urban cities. Adults in urban communities are better educated on average than adults in rural areas. Approximately 28 percent of urban adults hold college degrees in comparison to adults in rural areas where only 16 percent hold degrees (Nadel and Sagawa 2002). However, the school achievements of urban children are still not exceptional by any standard. More than 60 percent of urban children are not at proficient levels in reading, writing, or mathematics.

Urban children have more after-school and extended-day programs and their health care options are greater than in rural areas. However, since urban poor are highly concentrated within major cities in America, after-school programs are not adequately staffed and appropriate medical services are still limited. Once a family makes an income that is even one dollar above the poverty line, the family is no longer considered poor and therefore not entitled to aid or services (Chamberlin 2001), even though life in an urban city is three times more costly than in a rural area. The 1996 Personal Responsibility and Work Opportunity Reconciliation Act that reformed welfare has put single mothers into the workforce in record numbers (Duncan and Brooks-Gunn 2001). Welfare changes, including restraints on support for education and five-year limits on receiving financial support, have exacerbated the continual cycle of urban poverty. Because the majority of urban poor come from single-parent homes, generally headed by females, breaking the cycle of poverty becomes an almost impossible task when funding for child care and adult education is capped after a five-year period.

Within the past few years, similarities in rural and urban poverty have increased. First, both rural and urban poverty disproportionately affect children of color. The percentage of children in poverty has risen among African Americans, Hispanics, and American Indians. Second, both rural and urban children are involved in gangs, drugs, alcohol, and violence utilizing weapons. Gangs have become more and more prevalent in both rural and urban areas. Finally, rural and urban children live in single-parent, female-headed households. Approximately 28 percent of rural children and 31 percent of urban children lived in single-parent, female-headed households in the year 2000. The 1996 welfare reform bill has pushed both rural and urban mothers into the work force; however, the reductions in funding have created tremendous shortages in child care and medical care for themselves and their children. Self-sufficiency has become harder to attain (Biddle 2001; Nadel and Sagawa 2002).

THE LARGER CHALLENGE

Poverty is complex. Poverty is different in rural areas as compared to cities. It is different from state to state, region to region, and nation to nation. Connell (1994) points out that low income is generally viewed as a major indicator of poverty; however, a family's economic situation depends not just on unstable income but on more stable wealth, such as what is owned (Wilson 1996). Only looking at the poverty line, for example, is an inappropriate form of measurement because the distribution of wealth is not the same as the distribution of income. Although an American myth is that poverty exists only for African Americans who live in urban ghettos, the complex American reality is that poor people are not of one race, nor do the poor all live in cities. In terms of actual numbers, more white children are poor than African American or Latino children. In the United States, the child poverty rate is two to three times higher than that of other major Western industrialized nations; although the poverty rate is highest for African Americans (30 percent) and Latinos (29 percent), by international standards, it is also exceptionally high for white children (13 percent) (Lu 2003, 1). Poverty rates are even higher for children under age six (33 percent for African American, 33 percent for Latinos, and 15 percent for whites). One of five children under six lives in poverty. Child poverty peaked in 1993, and declined until 2001. According to the National Center for Children in Poverty (Lu 2003, 1), "The increase from 2000 to 2001 is statistically significant. Many of the concerns of the 'near poor' low-income families overlap with those of the poor, such as the need for well-paying jobs and access to affordable quality child care and health care." As stated previously, altogether about 27 million American children (38 percent) live in low-income families.

Clearly, the programs developed to eradicate poverty have not overcome it. According to Chamberlin (2001), the reason for this failure has to do with the fact that the individuals who developed all the policies did not recognize that the word *poverty* has another meaning. "Poverty also refers to a social arrangement by which the poor, while providing essential needs of the non-poor, receive wages that are less than it costs them to live. This is systemic poverty and it is the domain of the employed poor" (21). Chamberlin believes we will not overcome poverty—through education, or any other means—as long as the nonpoor continue to depend on the poor to perform low-paying, low-status jobs. Poverty becomes cyclical because one-third of the children in this country live in households that are poor.

According to Chamberlin (2001), the existence of stereotypes about poverty in the United States represents a failure of the educational system. He writes, "Because poverty is frequently met by indifference, accepting things as they are, and denigrating those on whom we depend, it is clear that most do not know how our system functions in relation to those at the bottom. They do not know because it has never been part of their education" (69). He calls upon educators of leaders, teachers, and the general public to accept the challenge of learning and teaching about the complexity of poverty, particularly its broader structural and systemic causes. Speaking specifically of those of us in the professions, Chamberlin writes, "The absence of the study of poverty in their professional preparation is one reason why we all share in perpetuating injustice toward the poor" (2001, 77). He challenges us to move our attention from "what poverty does to the poor to what poverty does to us, the non-poor" (69) so that we may understand how poverty threatens all of us. Our book is written in that same spirit.

OVERVIEW OF THE BOOK

In this chapter, we have highlighted issues associated with leadership in high-poverty schools and the complexities of poverty. Following this introduction, within chapters 2 and 3 are stories of dynamic, caring, passionate, and committed educational leaders of high-performing, high-poverty elementary schools. We believe readers who reflect on their heartwarming and inspiring personal and professional stories may become more effective educational leaders and advocates for children who live in poverty. Based on her case study research and written by Lyman, chapter 2 tells the story and shares the successes of Aurthur Perkins, principal of Harrison Primary School in Peoria, Illinois. Similarly, based on case study research and written by Villani, chapter 3 features the story and successes of Carmen Perez-Dickson, principal of Newfield School in Bridgeport, Connecticut. Chapter 4 presents a comparison of these two schools and of the best leadership practices of these two exemplary principals.

Beginning with chapter 5 we shift to the larger context of the case studies. In the context of the achievement gap, we examine previous research about best leadership practices for high-performing, high-poverty schools. In chapter 6 we explore the concept of deficit thinking. We present beliefs and attitudes about poverty encountered in our research with educators. We discuss from theoretical and practical perspectives how beliefs and attitudes about children and families living in poverty can be changed through processes of leadership, education, and experience. We argue that beliefs and attitudes are at the heart of best leadership practices for high-poverty schools. Improving learning and achievement in high-poverty schools requires a principal and staff who believe in the children and their potential. Finally, in chapter 7, we focus on how leaders can make a difference, the need for change, and the challenges of leadership for social justice. Principals must first educate their own attitudes before working to influence beliefs and attitudes of faculty and staff members. As you read the book, we invite you to begin examining your own beliefs and attitudes about poverty.

Chapter Two

Harrison School: "An Island of Goodness"

The extraordinary leadership of one African American woman principal facilitates high-quality teaching and learning for children and families served by an elementary school located on the grounds of a public housing project. Perhaps a better word to describe what Aurthur Mae Perkins does is *demand* high-quality learning and teaching. Against the backdrop of a continuing achievement gap for poor and minority students, this case study of a highly successful principal provides one answer to the question of which leadership patterns and practices foster learning for children in high-poverty schools. The school's program is research based and a work in progress. Aurthur Perkins is dynamic, forceful, and caring. Other words used to describe her have included innovative, spiritual, a fireball, passionate, intelligent, opinionated, kind, and miraculous, to list only a few. One teacher said, "You either love her or hate her." She has gathered a staff of professionals who all want to be at the school, who are a family, and who view their work together as a *calling*. Aurthur Perkins lives her values as she fights for her children to have the futures made possible by high-quality learning experiences. Her voice and other voices of diversity must be heard if we are to honor and learn from multiple leadership perspectives (Ah Nee-Benham and Cooper 1998; Dillard 1995; Lomotey 1989; Murtadha-Watts 1999; Reyes, Scribner, and Scribner 1999; Scheurich 1998; Quint 1994).

The purpose of my qualitative case study was to explore how the leadership patterns and practices of one principal have contributed to a successful learning environment in a high-poverty elementary school. In this chapter, I describe and reflect on what I learned. I spent a total of eighty-five hours on twelve different Thursdays from January through April 2002 with Perkins, principal of Harrison Primary School in Peoria, Illinois. During my first five visits, I shadowed Perkins and took field notes. During the next five visits, I combined observation with interviews of nineteen staff members, ranging from teachers to others in a wide variety of roles. All the taped interviews were transcribed. During the two final visits, I spent focused time in classrooms of every teacher I interviewed, and conducted one final interview with Perkins. Additionally, staff members completed written surveys designed to ascertain their perspectives on educating children from low-income families.

LEARNING SUCCESSES AT HARRISON: MEETING DEVELOPMENTAL NEEDS

Harrison Primary School, once a K–8 building, sits where it was built a hundred years ago. The 1901 three-story structure features numerous additions and extensions constructed over the years, ambling out from its central core. The successes of the school are exceptional considering that Harrison is located on the grounds of a public housing project in one of the poorest areas in Peoria. The average annual income for a Harrison Homes household is calculated by the Peoria Housing Authority to be $5,217. Harrison normally enrolls 475 children in pre-K programs through fourth grade. During the semester of my research, the school also had a fifth-grade pilot project classroom. A total of 99.7 percent of the children were classified as low income, with 3.3 percent having limited English proficiency and 10.2 percent chronically truant. The mobility rate was 52.6 percent. Racial/ethnic demographics of the students were 7.2 percent non-Hispanic white, 89.3 percent African American, and 2.3 percent Hispanic. At the time of my research, the school had, including the principal, a total of sixty-nine faculty and staff. There were twenty-six full-time pre-K–5 classroom teachers, six special education teachers, one ESL teacher, one speech and language pathologist, thirteen teaching assistant/aides, one librarian, two secretaries, eight cafeteria workers, four custodians, and six full- and part-time specialists assigned from the central office. These included two social workers, two psychologists, a nurse, and a secretary. Of the total staff of sixty-nine persons, twenty-three of them (or 33 percent) are members of a minority group (twenty-two

African Americans and one Hispanic). Of the thirty-nine certified teaching and professional staff, a total of eight persons (or 20.5 percent) are racial/ethnic minorities. Families living in the Harrison Homes public housing project include around 600 youth under the age of twenty, with 281 of those five or under. Children from the project and surrounding neighborhood attend the school. The project includes blocks of two-story brick apartments, many of which are completely vacant with boarded-up doors and windows. A police car is not an uncommon sight. In this high crime part of town, the school doors are nevertheless unchained. One teacher described the school aptly with the words "an island of goodness in a really hard place."

Although twelve of the thirty-seven schools in Peoria were on the Illinois academic watch list at the time of my research because of unacceptable levels of student achievement on state tests, Harrison was not one of them. The mission statement of the school suggests why: "We are dedicated to the developmental needs of the whole child. Through professional development and high expectations, students will be engaged in active, risk-free learning. Students will develop habits that will prepare them to be lifelong learners and productive citizens." Perkins and the staff have developed and implemented a wide range of educational programs and supportive services for the children and their families. Listing them all would be impossible, but they include a multifaceted 21st Century grant after-school program; a community volunteer program with a coordinator and fifty regular volunteers; a partnership with Bradley University that brings college students taking part in the *America Reads* program into the building regularly as tutors; many resources for the school and families from the six Adopt-a-School partners; school uniforms and special funds available if families need help in purchasing them; an in-school health center; emergency funds that provide needy children with glasses and medicine; a childcare room for mothers participating in the classes associated with the unique Growing Together program; a washer and dryer to support the child-care program and provide clean clothes for other children as needed; a reserve of food, clothing, shoes, formula, and diapers that are given to families in need; a holiday food basket program; a comprehensive educational component for family members; a variety of orderly procedures for the children to follow in the classrooms, halls, lunchroom, and playground; incorporation of technology with computer programs such as Breakthrough to Literacy; an instructional focus on engaged learning; departmentalized third- and fourth-grade classrooms; an English as a second language (ESL) staff member and classroom; the Second Step violence prevention curriculum; and the Harrison Initiative for Language Learning, which includes a unique, classroom-based phonemic awareness program.

Harrison students have been much more successful than might be expected on standardized state tests. For example, on the 2000 Illinois Standards Achievement Test (ISAT), 66 percent of third graders at Harrison met or exceeded the state standards for math, 54 percent met or exceeded the state standards for reading, and 70 percent met or exceeded the state standards for writing. Corresponding numbers for the 2001 ISAT tests were 55 percent in math, 64 percent in reading, and 69 percent for writing. Overall student achievement, when collapsing the scores from the subject area tests in third and fourth grades, averaged 52 percent meeting or exceeding state standards in 1998–1999, 57 percent in 1999–2000, and 56 percent in 2000–2001. Although scores on standardized tests represent only one measure of student learning, it is the measure making the news as principals in all states struggle with the challenge of raising students' achievement test scores. Interestingly, when asked to share a Harrison success story, half of the staff interviewed told stories of parents. Most of the stories were about how the parents took increasingly better care of their children as a result of interactions with the school staff and had grown into more responsible adults in a variety of ways, including going back to school themselves. Success stories about students were about increases in self-esteem, improved behaviors, and even the emergence of giftedness. No one mentioned test scores.

MEET THE PRINCIPAL: AURTHUR MAE PERKINS

Aurthur Mae Perkins became the principal of Harrison Primary School in 1992, having taught kindergarten at the school since 1983. She spent her first ten years in Richmond, Indiana, in a large extended African American family whose members supported each other through struggles and hard times. She was one of only a few girls in the large group of cousins and describes herself as having been a "bossy" young girl who liked to take charge of things. She liked to organize the neighborhood children to produce plays and then charge admission. Although she did not really enjoy school, she was a straight-A student with an uncanny love of reading. Except for one fight, she doesn't remember being in trouble in school, just not interested. An excellent student, in fact, Aurthur's reading skills were so advanced she was continually moved along in Richmond and would probably have graduated at age fifteen if the family had remained there. Aurthur's father, a laborer, was never really in the home. When she was about ten, her family moved to Macomb, Illinois, in search of work opportunities. They stayed for a year before moving to Peoria. In Macomb she remembers an outhouse, an old potbellied stove, and one great big open room that contained beds, chairs, tables—really, everything the family had.

A firstborn child, Aurthur lived with her hardworking mother and two brothers in Peoria. Life in Peoria involved frequent moves as the family struggled for resources. She dropped out of school in eighth grade at age thirteen when she had a baby. For a time, after Aurthur had the baby and her mother started to have heart problems, the family lived in a housing project. They even moved back to Richmond temporarily, but decided to return to the larger community of Peoria. Aurthur learned much from her resourceful mother, a college graduate who could always figure out how to make things work well. Her mother had run a day-care center in Indiana. In Peoria she worked as the first black supervisor of the custodial staff at OSF Saint Francis Hospital, and later moved into supervisory positions in Peoria restaurants. From the example and strong support of her mother, Aurthur absorbed the value of work. Life was challenging, but neither she nor her mother ever accepted welfare. Aurthur helped provide a living for the family. Her jobs always involved working with people.

Eventually she assumed the responsibility of caring for her brothers and mother after heart disease left her mother too ill to work. Today at age sixty-four, Aurthur Perkins has been married for fifty years and has raised seven children, six sons and one daughter. Aurthur has served in leadership roles in her church and the community, including the Peoria Public Library Board and the Peoria Housing Authority. She is a powerful voice in the African American community. Volunteerism led her to resume her own formal education. A volunteer tutor at a school attended by her own children, Perkins became outraged that so many African American children could not read and no one seemed to care. Determined to do something about this injustice, she went

2.1. Aurthur Perkins pauses for a picture in front of the floor-to-ceiling monthly calendar that dominates the wall across from the office.

back to school in her late thirties to get her GED. She had two sons in college at the time. She continued with higher education until she earned a B.S. in elementary education from Bradley University in Peoria in 1982. After a year of substituting, she began her teaching career at Harrison as a pre-K teacher, moving into the kindergarten classroom after a year. She earned an M.A. in educational administration from Bradley University in 1990. Reflecting on her almost twenty years at Harrison, she said, "This is where my heart was, my roots were here. I came from a project myself, and I felt a kinship to the people of this area, this school. It just felt like this was home to me."

The Setting

Most visitors to the school park along the west edge and enter double doors on the side of the building. A door at the end of the small entryway leads into the main hall of the school. A wide hallway extends straight ahead, as well as to the left and right. The floors are shiny linoleum. The walls are brown brick halfway up, with cream-colored paint on walls reaching to the high ceiling. Fluorescent light fixtures suspended from the fifteen-foot-high ceiling span the hall every ten feet or so and provide lots of illumination for the displays of student work as well as artifacts of the school's history. The principal's office is to the right. Directly across from the door into the office is a huge calendar for the month, approximately eighteen feet wide and twelve feet high. The collage style calendar is colorful, with construction paper shapes serving as backdrops for reminders of events, guests, and meetings, as well as historical events and holidays. The calendar is different every month.

The main office is the nerve center of the school. The front counter usually holds materials for the teachers, mail, attendance reports, and a coffee pot. Behind the front counter is a cluster of filing cabinets, a copier, two

2.2. *Harrison School is a century old at its core, with newer additions extending out in several directions from the original building.*

computer desk areas, a couple of extra chairs, and a conspicuous window
air conditioner—all framed by high windows with plaid curtains. Posters
with inspirational messages cover the walls. At any given time, children,
staff, and visitors come in and out of the office for a myriad of reasons.
Someone is usually on the phone or calling a person to the phone. The office is seldom quiet, and frequently the loudest voice in the room belongs to
the principal. In fact, there is nothing quiet about Aurthur Perkins, including her clothes. Always impeccably dressed, a short but imposing woman,
she wears colorful, flowing clothes with flair. Jewelry and shoes always
match. Her carefully groomed hair is cut close to her head. Her eyes flash.
She laughs easily and often. She frequently looks seriously determined. The
day of my first observation she wore the required uniform colors. Her loose-
fitting, tunic-length royal blue sweater was velour, topped with a gold neck-
lace. Her long black skirt hung almost to the ground, not quite hiding the
flat black shoes. My first day at Harrison provided much food for thought.
Recounting highlights gives a glimpse of Perkins's leadership practices.

A Typical Day

The school day at Harrison began with all the children gathering in the gym,
sitting on the floor in groups by grade level. In the gym with the children,
Perkins used the time to make announcements, hand out compliments, and
reinforce the procedures that govern student behavior. Then, fifteen minutes
before the school day actually began, each teacher came to the gym and
each classroom group left with its teacher to work for the first hour of the
day with the Harrison Initiative for Language Learning curriculum, math
skills, and writing exercises. The children walked quietly in single file with
their hands clasped behind their backs, one of the school's procedures.
Perkins's approach with the children in the gym and throughout the day was
very personal, a strong matriarchal style with no-nonsense language. She
threw her considerable energy into demanding good behavior from the children, sometimes threatening and often speaking like a scolding mother. "I
am disappointed in you. You should be ashamed of yourself," I heard her
say more than once. She also spoke consistently to the children of the importance of their choices, saying often, "I am hard on you because I love
you." She teaches them how to think through their behaviors, affirming their
worth, and giving hugs as freely as she gives scoldings. Children leave her
office wanting to do better and knowing that she believes they can.

The children left the gym; by 8:45 on my first morning, Perkins alternated between greeting people in the hallways and talking in the office with the children, not yet officially late, who were still arriving. She admonished two boys to go home and get their mothers to come over and see her. She visited in her office with one mother and her child who had been hurt in a playground accident. Following that conference, she was on the phone in the outer office with the district's new director of research, arranging a meeting with him and principals she is mentoring to talk about the Iowa Test of Basic Skills (ITBS) scores. She talked and joked cordially with the man who was in the building doing the fire code inspection. She spent time on the phone talking with someone who wanted to make a donation to the school, and she talked with a person at the Peoria Housing Authority in an attempt to find an apartment for a young woman with six children who had been staying at the South Side Mission. All of these things happened before she made the morning announcements on the public address system. She had a student take the microphone to lead all the students in the pledge of allegiance and this personal pledge recited in unison every day: "I believe in myself and my ability to do my best at all times, not just today. I will not waste today because this day will not come again." After the pledge and the lunch menu, she called the two students who were having birthdays to come down to the office. When they arrived each got a hug and a treat.

One of the boys who had been sent home arrived with his mother. Perkins called the child's teacher to come to the office also and I observed the emotional conference that ensued. At one point Perkins said to the mother, "I have to push both of you. You need to be back in school yourself. It is not easy. You've got to push yourself. It is important for you to get back into the GED program. Education is the key. We need to have your support. Get involved with the programs for parents. Get your child in the after-school programs. If he sees you not trying, then why should he try? He wants to be here and do well but he needs your support."

Aurthur handed the tearful mother a Kleenex and continued, "I'm being hard on you because we want you to succeed. We care about you." She thanked the teacher for coming and the boy and his teacher went off to class. Then she thanked the parent for coming and again encouraged her to try harder for the sake of her boy. She is not reluctant to take such a tough approach with parents, perhaps because she has walked in their shoes.

From then until noon, one thing after another transpired in the office as children, teachers, and parents were in and out, each with a need to which

Perkins responded. The backdrop of all this activity was joking, laughter, and an easy rapport. During the last hour of the morning, Perkins toured the first- and second-floor classrooms, as is her custom. She is in and out of the classrooms daily. Coming back to the office, we heard terrible yelling in the main hall, and she immediately took over with a fourth-grade boy who had become uncontrollably angry with a teacher. She talked him through the anger by validating it, but insisted that he settle himself down, stop acting crazy. She said, "I know you are angry. But you

2.3.   In addition to a well-equipped computer lab, every classroom at Harrison has computers so that a teacher can help students individually.

can't blame us for the problems you have. You should not have to cook your own dinner. You should not have to wash your own clothes and take care of your little brothers and sisters. But it's not my fault. I am only trying to love and help you. You scared the little children with your yelling. You can't disturb the whole school when you get mad."

He finally was able to calm down as she continued to talk and reason quietly but firmly with him. Then the three of us went into the cafeteria to have lunch together. We sat at one end of the long tables and she continued her conversation with the boy, expressing her hopes and care for him. At one point, he asked politely if he could get her another serving of something, and she said, "Yes, of course, that would be very nice." After lunch she sent him back to class with a renewed soul, and we continued our tour of the classrooms.

In every room, Perkins interacted with the children and teachers as I took lots of notes about the learning activities occurring. By the time the classroom visits concluded, I had a good outline of the particular programs and procedures that Perkins and the staff have developed and implemented to meet the learning needs of the children. I also had a list of questions that I spent the next few months trying to answer. Back in the office, Perkins finally had about fifteen minutes of down time before making the 3:00 P.M. announcements. After the announcements, teachers walked the children who were leaving to the outside doorways. About 200 children stayed at the school and gathered in the gym for snacks before the after-school programs funded by a 21st Century grant began. In addition to various tutoring choices, the thirty-five options included art, ballet, orchestra, chorus, dance, karate, 4-H, basketball, Scouting programs, keyboarding, sewing, Spanish, tumbling, young authors, and more. When I left the school about 5:30, Perkins was still there, and would be until all the children left around 6:00.

LEADERSHIP PATTERNS AND PRACTICES

Field notes at the end of my first day at Harrison included the observation that Perkins's leadership was about both facilitating and demanding. I recorded the words *loving* and *warm*, but also *firm* and *strict* to describe her. My dominant images were of her easy rapport with others, of an office filled with people, joking, and laughter. I noted that she put in a long day and engaged in lots of one-on-one work with students, staff, and parents. Perkins's personal office usually presents a many-layered picture of controlled chaos. The large conference table dominating the room is seldom clear, used more as a desk than the actual large wooden desk behind which Perkins rarely sits. Teaching materials, cookies and treats, mail, books, file folders, reports, and other works in progress look at home on the conference table. Staff seem at home coming in and out of her office for treats from the candy basket. Perkins herself is more at home in the front office, the hallways, or the classrooms. Staff interview responses as well as additional days of observation and conversation with Perkins gave me a clearer look at her leadership patterns and practices.

Staff Interview Responses

Working from an interview guide, I spoke with nineteen persons (or 28 percent of the total staff) in interviews lasting from thirty to sixty minutes. Perkins and I selected the interviewees to be representative of a range of roles and viewpoints. The group included one teacher from each grade level (six); the science, physical education, computers/music, and ESL teachers (four); the speech pathologist (one); two pre-K teachers and an aide (three); a caseworker with the truancy prevention program, the coordinator of parent education and after-school programs, and a parent who works in the child-care room (three); and a custodian and the cafeteria manager (two). Of the interviewees, thirteen (or 68 percent) were certified teachers or professional staff members. All of the interviews were taped with permission and transcribed. Responses to three of the questions will be presented in this chapter, with the remaining questions discussed in following chapters. Two of the interview questions focused on leadership.

How do faculty and staff feel supported by the leadership of Mrs. Perkins?
    A major theme of the responses to this question, "How does the leadership of Mrs. Perkins support your work?" was what I call the *relational approach* of Perkins as a leader. Comments supporting the theme included how much she appreciates them, how they value her willingness to communicate with them, how she always backs them up, and how she has facilitated a subculture of teacher leaders. For example, one spoke of how "she schedules time for us to meet with each other." As one teacher ex-

plained, she has "an open door policy" and has been good at "hiring a staff that has good chemistry." One person expressed that Perkins was "supportive of individuality." Another said she is "supportive of my doing what I need to do for students and families. She trusts me to make professional judgments." Four specifically mentioned how she "backs us up all the time." Three highlighted her skills in building relationships with the parents, particularly in getting them to come to school, as well as her practice of making and encouraging the teachers to make home visits. In general, interviewees spoke of Perkins as caring about them, believing in them, listening to them, and being understanding. For example, said one first-year teacher, "She helped me get my classroom under control, a real issue for me in the beginning of the year. When I have cried in discouragement she has encouraged me and listened, not chastised me. When I have had problems she was always there and said 'okay, let's deal with this.' She has called parents for me and her strong personality has helped me get the students where they need to be."

A second major theme was her willingness to *take charge*. For example, she is "directive" said one; "she required teachers to do the phonemic awareness," said another; "she pushed me or I never would have written that first grant," another confessed; and finally, "she weeds out weak teachers." Associated with the "take charge" theme, three teachers spoke of her compelling way of getting things done. Others mentioned how she continually supports them with classroom materials, works with children who have difficult discipline issues, and provides programs to meet the children's needs. For example, one teacher said, "She makes sure we have everything we need in our classroom. If we need any type of materials to help us teach the children, she will make sure that we have it. She is always there for you, no matter what. She is a caring person, she loves, but yet she has that discipline, that structure. She wants everything done in order and in the right way."

Four other themes emerged from the responses. The first of these was her "above and beyond" effort, her hard work, how she spends long hours at the school, is willing to go outside the norm, and is always "fighting for what we need," including technology. One teacher aptly summed up these practices, "She is 100 percent there." A second category was responses dealing with her "clear vision and high expectations." Two final categories are that she is seen as an exemplar or role model, and she keeps up with research,

Table 2.1. Summary of Themes in Responses to First Interview Question about Leadership

Response Frequency*	Themes in Interview Responses
13	She takes a relational approach with staff and parents.
10	She is willing to take charge.
4	She gives above-and-beyond effort.
3	She has a clear vision and high expectations.
2	She is an exemplar and role model.
2	She gives informed support to innovation.

*N = 19

thereby encouraging risk taking and innovation. Table 2.1 summarizes the themes that emerged from content analysis of responses to the question "How does the leadership of Mrs. Perkins support your work?"

How would you describe Mrs. Perkins as a leader?

The second interview question about leadership, "If you could only use three words, how would you describe Mrs. Perkins as a leader?" was asked toward the end of each interview. The most frequently used word to describe Perkins was *caring*, offered by four people. The two words that tied for second, each offered three times, were *strong* and *supportive*. These most frequently offered words suggest the same two primary patterns that emerged in analysis of the responses to the first interview question about Perkins's leadership: that she takes a *relational approach* (caring and supportive) and that she has the ability to *take charge* (strong).

Further analysis of the fifty-two words offered clearly identifies the same two primary themes that emerged in responses to the question of "How does the leadership of Mrs. Perkins support your work?" Half of the fifty-two words are either about her relational approach or her take-charge ability. For example, fourteen words describe her relational approach—caring (4), supportive (3), compassionate (2), giving, helpful, sincere, kind, and understanding. Another twelve words describe aspects of the take-charge dimension of her leadership—strong (3), innovative (2), dedicated, persuasive, high expectations, tough, bossy, visionary, authoritative.

Four additional categories emerged that also match patterns identified in responses to the first question about leadership. One category is a group of nine words that describe energy-related qualities of personality that make possible her above-and-beyond effort—passionate (2), energetic (2), dynamic, fireball, direct, enthusiastic, a go-getter. Another group of four words acknowledges Perkins as a leader whose spiritual calling supports her clear vision and high expectations—religious, godly, Christian values, spiritual. Another category contains seven words referring to qualities of mind that incline her to innovation and risk taking—intelligent (2), knowledgeable (2), thoughtful, professional, and opinionated. In the final group are six terms that describe the larger-than-life qualities that make her an exemplar—extraordinary, spectacular, magnificent, miraculous, role model, mother of all. Table 2.2 summarizes the themes that emerged from the interview question about what three words best describe Perkins as a leader.

When asked how she thought others would describe her, Perkins chose the words dynamic, forceful, and caring. When asked why those adjectives, she answered:

> I think *dynamic* because I am able to break through the tough situations, you know, like dynamite. I get to where I need to go without a lot of dallying around. I get through. And then the *forceful* part is that I will not give up. It is going to work because this is the way it should be. It's like cod liver oil. You may not want to take it, but once you do then you'll find out that it will work. And then comes the *caring* part, when I pick up the pieces that I sometimes have to pick up because of the dynamic persistence I may have used getting to the bottom of a situation. The caring part is there at the beginning and at the end, but they don't always see that first. They don't always get that!

Her words reveal a high level of self-awareness and are essentially congruent with how staff members who were interviewed view her as a leader. Her words echo in reverse order the top two patterns they described: she

Table 2.2. Summary of Categories in Responses to Second Interview Question about Leadership

Response Frequency*	Categories in Interview Responses to "What three words describe Mrs. Perkins as a leader?"**
14	Relational approach
12	Take-charge ability
9	Personal dynamism
4	Spiritual values
7	Qualities of mind
6	Larger than life

*N = 19
**Total number of words = 52

takes a *relational approach* (caring) and she is willing to *take charge* (dynamic, forceful).

Why is Harrison such an outstanding school?

In response to the final interview question, "Is there anything else you can tell me about why Harrison is such an outstanding school?," most persons interviewed clearly stated that the school has been so successful because of the strong focus on providing emotional support to the children, their families, and each other. The majority spoke of the caring, giving, dedicated, and hardworking staff; the strength and high expectations of Mrs. Perkins; and the teamwork and communication among the staff and Mrs. Perkins. Said one teacher, "Everyone is here for the kids. It is a cause. Have you seen our test scores, have you seen what we are doing? I think that God wants me to be here. Nobody is here just to collect a paycheck." Another teacher said it this way:

> We go the extra mile to reach a parent or child, to make them see that we care and that they can succeed. You put so many strong-willed, compassionate people together and you are going to have success. I really think that our success has been our compassion, a dedication to try something different and to try it as a group. When we started collaborating, whether within our grade level or among grade levels we saw that the children were making gains. I think you need cohesiveness within your group, and I don't think that all schools have that. Minds working together make a greater impact.

Several singled out Mrs. Perkins as the reason for the school's success. One mentioned how "she pushes us to want to be the best," and how she has built the teamwork through a combination of communication, pressure, and support. One teacher said, "Mrs. Perkins helps make it a great place just because of who she is and what she expects. She expects that these kids perform, that they do well, and that the teachers are teaching what they need to be teaching, and that is what she gets." The teachers and staff members interviewed clearly see the whole school as going the extra mile. One person described the school as "an island of goodness." Several spoke of the emotional and academic support provided for the students, mentioning the desire of staff for the students to succeed, staff members' compassion, and how staff members value the parents. For example, a teacher's aide said, "The parents come and they learn with the children.

The parents are always thought of first in this building. Mrs. Perkins is always pushing for what the parents want. The parents are respected in this building." Academic or program features were not ignored as reasons for the school's success. Those mentioned included the focus on language through phonemic awareness instruction and other aspects of the Harrison Initiative for Language Learning, teachers spending time on language each day, children in the classroom fifteen minutes early, consistent expectations, direct instruction, structure, uniforms, the early childhood wing, parental programs, teachers who make learning interesting, and outside people coming to the school.

Perkins's actions as a leader display her deep commitment to children and their learning. She sees her work at Harrison as a calling. Her words validate the spiritual dimension of her leadership described by the staff. "We believe in angels and ask for prayer. I have never heard any concern expressed about someone saying 'I prayed about it,'" Perkins said. She is committed to telling the truth "because God is always listening to my mouth." Asked specifically about values, she responded:

> I value life, I respect life, and I respect the lives of others. I believe in treating people like I want to be treated. I believe in giving people freedom to do what they need to do. Everybody is an individual. I don't want anyone to be a clone of someone else. We're all different and unique and that's the way God made us. . . . This speaks to me about how diverse He is. And I think this is why it is important to respect the diversity in people and allow people to be themselves. My values are steeped in everything I do. I believe in the power of prayer, and I believe that prayer guides the school and guides everything that I do, and guides the people that are in this school. I also believe that everyone in the school is here on a mission. They're assigned here for a period in time just as I am. Then you go off the stage. And so I value always all of the input and all of the things they bring continually.

Murtadha-Watts explains how "African American women in leadership positions often draw upon profound historical traditions of inner spiritual strength as well as an activist ethic of risk/urgency" (1999, 155–56). In her study of twenty-five African American women in leadership roles, she found that many "refer to spirituality as their source of strength and guidance" (156). Perkins's description of herself as a praying woman always seeking higher guidance, and her conviction that she and everyone else at the school are on a mission place her within this tradition of African American women leaders who find guidance and strength in their religious beliefs.

I was shadowing Perkins one day when a local television reporter was at the school to cover the visit of the lieutenant governor. Finished with that interview, he then turned his camera on Perkins. He began the interview with the observation that the school was more decorated with students' work than other schools he had visited. Then he asked her why Harrison was such a star-quality school. Perkins's reply was immediate: "It's the excellent staff I have. We work together. We are committed to the education of the children and their families. We have a vision of what things can be. We celebrate the success stories. We do a lot of unique things. We know we have to do things a different way to get the results we get." Her response is reflective of a comment by a staff member about how Perkins gives them all the credit and "sings their praises wherever she goes."

OBSERVATIONS ABOUT LESS-SUCCESSFUL, HIGH-POVERTY SCHOOLS

When I asked Perkins how Harrison is different from less-successful, high-poverty schools, she had clear opinions. "Every school cannot be the same. I don't think that my school is the same as any other school, but I do think some of the strategies that we use at Harrison can be duplicated and make a difference in the lives of children," she stated unequivocally. Asked what she has observed in less-successful schools, Perkins offered five observations. They include principals who plan rather than do, who do not know the research, who don't work with their teachers, who don't have caring relationships with staff, and who deal with discipline differently than she does.

Observation One

Perkins's first statement was, "I see way too much planning and not enough doing." Perkins believes that principals need to work hard at doing what is needed for the children. "Kids come in behind but can get caught up. The programs need to be innovative, with the principal acting as a risk taker, being creative, and finding new programs," she explained. One of her first actions as a new principal was to require teachers to get to know their students as individuals. She went into classrooms the second week of class and asked each teacher how many of their children they really knew. Most of them said, "I don't know." So she explained that their first job was to get to know them, and to get to know them well.

> They have names, they have home lives, and it is time to get to know them as individuals. You don't just lump them all together and call them a group, second graders or third graders. These are individuals, with individual needs, and individual hurts. You've got to know them, you've got to know what they know, know what their strengths are. You've got to know what their weaknesses are. You've got to know that total child. You must know what motivates a child, why a child is not motivated, why a child is sleeping in class.

From this charge came all the other positive changes in the building, Perkins believes. "When they got to know the children as individuals they began to involve themselves in truly educating these children."

Perkins makes decisions with confidence. The sign on her office door, "Because I said so," both does and doesn't explain Perkins as a leader. Quite decisive and able to take charge, she is also a reflective and inclusive decision maker. Before she makes a major decision, she usually calls a couple of teachers in "to bounce some things around." She likes to call in two completely different people, but ones who will tell her the truth. She explained, "Any decision that is going to change the school, I always have a team of people with me. I don't do a lot of that by myself, and the bottom line is when I have to do it I have to do it. But I'm interested in your voice. Whether it is a good or a bad decision I have to make the final decision. I'll make it and move on." She does not worry too much about making bad decisions because, as she puts it, "I am a praying woman. I'm always praying. I'm always seeking higher guidance, and so therefore, if I say or do anything I am not expecting it to turn out wrong. And I'm not expecting to say or do something that would make everybody else around me uncomfortable." Perkins is a leader who believes in the wisdom of the group and in her own wisdom, guided by prayer. "I'm ready to charge ahead with what I feel is right for the children. That's number one, that the students be given what they need; and then number two is that the staff is ready to be on board with what I'm doing; and number three, the parents. So I'm very comfortable with what I do. I have confidence in myself," she concluded.

Observation Two

Perkins was particularly adamant in saying, "I talk with principals who do not seem to know the research about teaching and learning, particularly about what children living in poverty need to be academically successful." Perkins reads professional journals and attends conferences. She pays attention to research. If something would be good for her children, she will make it happen at Harrison. When asked about research, she replied that the most important research findings utilized at Harrison have been about phonemic awareness, parent involvement, and students' engagement in the classroom through relationships with the teachers. A prime example of how Perkins has brought about application of research findings is the classroom teacher-delivered phonemic awareness program that has been underway since 1994. Research findings shared with Perkins by speech and language pathologist Patricia Lindberg about the importance of phonemic awareness for reading success led to the development of the Harrison Initiative for Language Learning. Understanding the implications of the research, Perkins pushed Lindberg to write a grant to develop a program and Lindberg has become a major partner in the leadership of the school (Lyman 2003). The major components of today's comprehensive Harrison Initiative for Language Learning are decoding (including phonemic awareness), comprehension, and pragmatic skills. During the 1994–1995 academic year, Lindberg worked with the team of kindergarten teachers to develop a classroom-based phonemic awareness program. Lindberg provided the training and did the curriculum writing while the teachers came up with the activities to put the research about how phonemic awareness enhances reading into practice. Grant money paid for substitutes as well as stipends so that the kindergarten teachers were able to meet with Lindberg for a half day weekly to develop these new techniques and materials for enhancing language skills.

Wanting a base of data from which to document success of the new curriculum, Lindberg gave all kindergarten students a diagnostic test in the spring of 1994. Scores from the Test of Awareness of Language Segments

(TALS) showed that at the end of 1994 only 29 percent of the ninety-five students finishing kindergarten were ready for instruction in a regular basal reading series. By the spring of 1995, the new curriculum having been implemented as it was being developed, scores from the same test showed 59 percent of the ninety-two students completing kindergarten were ready for regular basal reader instruction. Every spring since 1995, continuing administration of the TALS has shown that from 73 percent to 79 percent of the students completing kindergarten are ready for a basal reading series.

The gains revealed by the TALS results were encouraging each year, but the real validation of the effectiveness of the program came with the state achievement test scores in the fall of 1999. The state of Illinois implemented the new Illinois Standards Achievement Test (ISAT) program in 1998–1999. Based on newly developed state curriculum standards, the ISAT test was considered to be more rigorous than the previous Illinois Goals Assessment Program (IGAP) tests. As reported in the *Peoria Journal Star*, "But while students at Harrison have previously struggled on other standardized tests, this year proved to be much better for the school" (Brown 1999). In math, 70 percent of the students met or exceeded the state standards, better than districtwide or statewide results. In reading, 51 percent met or exceeded the state standards as well. Brown elaborated, "Perkins credits much of the improvement to the Harrison Initiative for Language Learning, a reading and language program that was developed by school staff members and was implemented five years ago." As previously discussed, students from Harrison have continued to do well academically on the state tests.

Says Lindberg of the program, "I wish I had thought of this. I didn't. All I did was read the research and try to figure out how to apply it in a classroom situation. There was nothing in the research at the time we wrote our curriculum that showed this [phonemic awareness instruction] being done by teachers in a classroom situation." Preliminary analysis of the longitudinal data on the approximately one thousand children who have experienced the Harrison program "shows that children we had from the beginning make very good progress and maintain their progress." Summarizing the program, Lindberg wrote in a 1999 handbook published by the school district, "Encouraged by student achievement, teacher satisfaction, and positive test results, Harrison Staff has spent four-and-a-half years refining and extending the language curriculum to include grades pre-K through fourth. Furthermore, we are now not only working on language skills requisite to reading but also on prosocial language skills."

In addition to knowing the research and implementing innovative, research-based programs, Perkins also believes that principals must go into the classrooms regularly enough to assess the learning environment.

> I am throughout the building and I can observe and pick up and feel what is going on with the teachers just from that. I can see from their interactions with the children whether learning will be taking place. I know what a school should look like and what classrooms should look like when children are coming from high-poverty areas. A room needs to look good and bright and cheerful for the kids. It needs to be warm, cozy, and inviting to the children.

When I asked Perkins what she thought educators needed to do to assist children in poverty to succeed academically, she responded with a focus on raising self-esteem.

> You have to get by some things and one is low self-esteem. They have to know that they are worth something and will be accepted for who and what they are as individuals. You have to make them proud. The connection has to be made in the classroom so that throughout the school the teachers feel good about what they are doing and the children feel good about wanting to please the teachers and ultimately please me. That is the most important thing: to bring up that child's self-esteem.

Perkins stresses often to the staff that each of them can make a significant difference to the children, and that these children are worth it. "They each have a life and a future. That they come from bad backgrounds does not matter. They are not throwaway kids," she emphasizes. Perkins understands that when learning happens for the children from low-income families much more than a curriculum and standards are at work.

Observation Three

A third observation was, "I have found that other principals don't work with the teachers in any ongoing way." At Harrison, grade levels meet weekly and Perkins meets with a different grade level each week. Perkins sees these meetings, in addition to regular monthly faculty meetings, as essential. "I ask what the teachers need from me, focus discussion on where we are in terms of where we want to be, and ask for names of any failing students so that they may get help." Commitment to a collaborative, facilitative style is indicated in Perkins's practice of engaging in ongoing work with the teachers, her commitment to building a family of teacher leaders who have autonomy, and her inclusion of others in decision making. Central to Perkins's leadership success is her support of the dedicated staff, most of whom she has hired. Staff turnover has been minimal, in contrast to what the research says about teacher turnover being a major problem in many high-poverty schools. Faculty and staff stay at Harrison because even though they all work hard, they are committed to the mission of the school, they get lots of support from the principal, and they enjoy being part of the Harrison family. In an interview, one teacher fairly new to the school spoke about the importance of Perkins's high expectations and collaboration with faculty when she elaborated about how Harrison was different from a school where she had formerly taught.

> This school is more on track with student achievement. They know what needs to be done. I am required to work with my grade level. I am required to meet with Mrs. Perkins at our grade-level meetings to see what we are doing. Everybody is required to do the same thing the first hour of the day, the phonemic awareness and our math drills and writing every morning. I felt more like I was babysitting at my other school. Here I am expected to hold high expectations even though they don't eat supper the night before. They deserve me to teach them just like my kids are taught in a white middle-class neighborhood. At my other school I was not expected to know so much about all my kids, and I wasn't expected to turn in progress reports every time. I was not expected to hand in lesson plans, and those kinds of things are expected of me now. I don't think home visits were done there, certainly not spur of the moment like the one you went on with Mrs. Perkins and me.

Observation Four

Perkins observed that in other less-successful schools, "I do not see joking and caring relationships between staff members and their principals." In the course of a day, Perkins has fun with people, holding both joking and serious conversations about a whole range of topics. Perkins has been at Harrison twenty years and loves every day she comes to work. "I love my staff, I love my children, I love the families, I love everything about it," she said. Speaking of the family atmosphere, Perkins said, "I want us to be a family, a happy family. I work very hard to promote that atmosphere. You don't find people every day that you can fight with, you can cry with, and you can laugh with." Perkins has a young staff and most of them have young children. As a mother herself, she understands that young children have lots of problems. She is flexible and quick to provide the support her teachers need to take care of their families, even if that means finding a substitute at the last minute or in the middle of the day.

Perkins has worked to build a family of teacher leaders who have autonomy. Perkins promotes teacher autonomy because she does not understand leadership to be about control. She said, in fact, "In some schools I see leadership missing. Instead of caring I see fear. I guess in some I see fear of not being recognized as 'the principal,' and that is the control part. They want to have some kind of control. I am not a control freak." Asked what she looks for when hiring a staff member for the school, Perkins described the capacity for that teacher to become part of the leadership. She elaborated:

> I am really looking for someone who at least appears to be strong, a self-starter. And eventually I look for them to take over a leadership role. So I don't sit on them. I let them have free rein. I try to give them an opportunity to use their gifts and let them flow. That is something I really enjoy about my school. All of them that want to lead can lead, those that want to follow can follow, and the rest can kind of just fit in the middle.

Observation Five

A final observation was, "I see other principals deal with discipline differently and use home visits infrequently." Perkins believes in providing personal, in-school discipline that combines caring and tough love. When confronted with misbehavior, the first choice of many principals is to suspend and send the student home. "That is my absolute last resort and used infrequently," Perkins explained. "I just don't do it." Instead, she provides discipline within the structure of school, including time sitting on the floor in the office for some. One morning when two girls were reported by their teacher to have behaved badly for a substitute the day before, Mrs. Perkins, the teacher, and I took the two girls with us and made two home visits. After Mrs. Perkins talked frankly with their mothers about their misbehaviors, we brought one girl back to school with us; the other was directed to take a bath and put on clean clothes, and then come back to school. Perkins has been quite successful in enlisting the cooperation and support of the parents regarding issues of behavior. She explained her philosophy of discipline within the school structure:

Children in poverty areas want to be disciplined and structured, and they don't have enough of it. Some people think you are hurting them or their feelings when you set up parameters and procedures, but that is not the case at all. They need the structure. They know that they have no control and they need someone to be in charge of them, to keep them in control. They know they don't have any control at home, so they try teachers. "If you can do it then I will respect you. And if you can't I am kicking you aside too."

Helping the students become successful academically combines conveying that you believe in them, that they are worthy, and "because of that, here are some procedures we will follow," she explained.

As previously stated, Perkins's approach with the children is very personal, a strong matriarchal style with no-nonsense language often interspersed with tough language. She told me once that her goal with such language is "to disturb the disturbed," to get their attention. She and the staff know about and regularly see the attachment disorders that can afflict children who have suffered too many traumas in the first year or two of life. She has actively sought psychological help for severely troubled children. Perkins believes that the children and families need tough love, need to be required to take responsibility for themselves, their actions, and the consequences of their actions. She will do anything to help a person who is trying, but gives little sympathy to those who are not willing to try. "Some people think I'm mean," she told me. "I say what I think to children and adults. People know where I stand. I keep the focus on the learning of the children."

When two girls were brought into the office for fighting the first day I was there, Perkins's response followed a pattern I saw repeated over and over, whether the children fighting were girls or boys. First, she asked the girls to look at each other. Then she said to each one, "This is your sister. Do you want to see her dead? Then tell her what you are sorry for. Hug each other and say you are sorry. This is your sister." She insisted that they look at each other's faces, use words to say what they had done, be clear about what they were sorry about, and give each other a hug. The fight resolved, then she asked the two girls to go back to their classrooms and have a good day. I did not ever see this approach or some variation of it fail to bring peace. The results she gets in changed behaviors indicate that Perkins's scolding admonishments communicate with the children in culturally meaningful ways. With fighting and other misbehaviors, there are some repeat offenders, almost always children for whom something is going on at home, but usually the behaviors turn around because the children understand that they are respected and valued, and that Mrs. Perkins and their teachers want them to become somebody.

REFLECTION

Coexisting in Perkins's leadership practices are two primary patterns: taking a caring relational approach and being willing to take charge. I observed that she both facilitates and demands. I also observed the four additional patterns that emerged from analysis of the surveys and interview transcripts: the above-and-beyond effort of a dynamic, committed person; clear vision and high expectations that are anchored in spiritual values; informed and intelligent support of innovation; and her powerful role as an exemplar and model of success for the children and their families, who know she has been where they are.

Researchers individually and in teams have studied clusters of high-poverty schools where learning of students exceeds expectations. They have identified the commonalities of these schools in terms of components such as a curriculum aligned with standards, a strong focus on language, a culture of caring and high expectations, parent involvement, and strong leadership (Barth, Haycock, Jackson, Mora, Ruiz, Robinson, and Wilkins 1999; Carlson, Shagle-Shah, and Ramirez 1999; Carter 2002a, 2002b; Catania 2001; Haycock 2001; Johnson and Asera 1999; Riester, Pursch, and Skrla 2002; Scheurich 1998; Sebring and Bryk 2000). My case study research suggests that these components are also in place at Harrison Primary School and can be used to explain the school's successes. However, the central finding of this case study is that Aurthur Perkins's leadership success is a testimony to the combined power of support and pressure to change schools, particular high-poverty schools (Fullan 1999; Sebring and Bryk 2000). She is a seriously determined woman, both a thinker and a doer whose leadership illustrates Haberman's contention that "the connection between what star principals do and how they think about what they do cannot be broken" (1999, x). As a leader, Perkins is acknowledged for both her caring and her toughness. The children, their parents, faculty, and staff members experience both support and pressure.

Perkins's personal history and struggles with poverty have contributed to who she is and how she does things. Focusing an entire book on nine diverse women school leaders, Ah Nee-Benham and Cooper remind us that their stories "ground our understanding of leadership in culture and context, elements frequently missing in mainstream literature on leadership" (1998, 3). Perkins leads from her unique cultural and contextual understandings about the needs of children and families living in poverty. Although motivated to go back to school because of her outrage that so many African American children could not read and no one seemed to care, Perkins does not dwell on injustices. She said, "Yes, things were done to us that were bad and they are still being done. I've let that go. It is not a focus. I focus on what the children need. My mother pushed me and accepted no excuses."

Just as she has been shaped by her mother's values, so too does her commitment to children reflect the African American community's *Othermothering* tradition. As explained by Murtadha-Watts (1999), "Many black women leaders act as Othermothers, a responsiveness to family in the larger community, thinking not only of themselves and the children they may have birthed, but offering care for children who have not experienced the loving and fussing nurturance of family" (156). Perkins as an Othermother is inclusive, clearly extending her loving and fussing nurturance to all children.

It's about the children, not about us. I'm committed to the cause of the children, of all children, black or white, because the white ones that are poor are just like we are. I mean, they don't have the same opportunities either. So you give them a lift and show them that you care. I do not see children as black or white, and neither does my staff. They have been trained not to do that. If I hear any such discussion, I address it right away.

In January 2002, I was in a second grade classroom at Harrison School when a teacher led the children in a discussion about Dr. Martin Luther King's life and death. The children practiced taking turns talking by tossing the *talking ball* to each other. Eventually the teacher asked the children, "Why do you think someone shot Dr. King?" When the ball came around the circle to him, one boy said, "I think they killed him because of how he felt about the laws. He was trying to change the laws." A girl said, "Some people were mad and did not want to be friends." Finally, the ball went to a small, timid-looking girl who said with surprising strength, "I think he was killed because they did not want black people to start leading white people." I do not remember my time at Harrison without seeing her small bright face and hearing her heart-stopping, insightful words.

My review of case study research suggests that many successful leaders of high-poverty schools are African American and Hispanic. Many are women. It is past time to simply hear about the leadership patterns and practices of educational leaders who speak from a perspective of diversity. It is time to honor their voices by listening and following their lead.

Chapter Three

Newfield School: "Where Angels Soar"

Carmen Perez-Dickson is an energetic, caring, passionate, family-oriented leader. Carmen is strong in her beliefs and convictions. She demands that all children be treated with respect and dignity. She demands that all students are educated to the highest level of academic achievement that they can reach. Carmen is a principal in an urban school where the achievement gap for poor and minority students is a district focus. Carmen does not believe in a cause-and-effect relationship between being poor and the ability to learn. The following case study tells the story of a highly successful principal who has created a unique learning environment. Her philosophy and practices are based on educational research, years of experience, and inherent values that she received in her childhood. Carmen lives her convictions.

LEARNING SUCCESSES AT NEWFIELD: A TOTAL LEARNING COMMUNITY SCHOOL

Newfield School is a prekindergarten through third grade school in Bridgeport, Connecticut, an urban city in Fairfield County. An interesting description is provided by the principal in the annual strategic school profile written for the State Department of Education in Connecticut: "Newfield Elementary School is a small community-based school where we model, teach, and reinforce appropriate social behavior through the Pillars of Character. . . . Our staff members have developed an effective and productive partnership with all parents and several local agencies to improve healthy student development."

The school had a total enrollment of 188 students during the time of my research. The school has one administrator (the principal), thirteen full-time faculty, four paraprofessionals, a psychologist, and a speech/language therapist. The school also has one secretary, a custodian, three cafeteria workers, and a part-time homeschool coordinator. Of the professional staff members, 55 percent are from minority groups. The race/ethnicity breakdown for students is: 1.1 percent non-Hispanic white, 73.4 percent African American, and 25 percent Hispanic. The number of students who receive free or reduced lunch is 86.5 percent, as compared to the district average of 92.0 percent and the Connecticut average of 14.2 percent for K–3 schools. The number of students with a non-English home language is 11.2 percent compared to the district average of 31.1 percent and the state average of 4.9 percent for K–3 schools. The number of students who receive special education is 17.0 percent. Newfield School uses a schoolwide approach to compensatory education. Supplemental instructional services include in-class tutors for language arts and a summer school program.

Academically, students in Connecticut are first tested with the Connecticut Mastery Test at the beginning of fourth grade. The test is an assessment of the child's reading, writing, and mathematical abilities. Scores are reported based on the percentage of students who reach the state's goals for mastery. Students who completed Newfield School performed above the district average in all three areas: reading, writing, and mathematics. Although lower than the state average, their scores continue to rise. For example, the most recent CMT scores were those reported for the 2001 school year, which indicated that in reading, 54.0 percent of students from Newfield achieved mastery compared to 37.5 percent districtwide and 69.2 percent statewide. In writing, 69.8 percent achieved mastery, compared to 57.3 percent districtwide and 76.5 percent statewide; and in mathematics, 55.3 percent achieved mastery compared to 52.4 percent districtwide and 78.1 percent statewide.

Newfield's Mission

Teachers, staff, and the principal created Newfield's mission statement collaboratively. It encapsulates the strong beliefs and commitments of this school community:

Newfield School is a small pre-kindergarten through third grade school where Children are First! Our mission is to develop an effective partnership among all parents, community members and our staff members as stakeholders in our students' lives. Together, the stakeholders will work collaboratively to develop a positive learning community where all students will benefit from quality education in a secure and nurturing environment. As a result, our students will become lifelong learners and productive citizens that will empower their community through their many successes.

Newfield's Goals

Newfield School has five overarching goals. For each goal, there are specific performance standards, performance-based assessments, strategies, a clear statement as to the target population and resources needed, and a realistic timeline. The overarching goals are as follows:

- *Literacy*. Students will develop proficiency, confidence, and fluency in reading, writing, and speaking to meet the literacy demands of the twenty-first century.
- *Numeracy*. Students will use numbers to count, measure, compare, order, scale, locate, and label. They will use a variety of numerical representations to present, interpret, communicate, and connect various kinds of numerical information.
- *School Climate*. Staff members, students, and their families will model, teach, and reinforce Character Counts and conflict resolution strategies. Newfield School's Home/School Compact will be implemented to reinforce expectations for staff members, students, and parents.
- *Pupil Services*. Students will benefit from Student Assistance Team process through early identification and interventions to promote student academic and social success.
- *Parent/Community*. Newfield School staff members will continue to expand partnerships with parents/families and community agencies to assist positive student development.

Developed by the faculty and staff as a whole, each of these overarching goals has associated with it very specific, student-centered steps and strategies for successful accomplishment of the goal. A priority is focusing on what the student needs to understand and how best to achieve that understanding.

Additionally, a commitment to develop strong parent and community relationships exists. Some of the specific objectives for this commitment are parent programs, parent meetings and trips, and partnerships with the local church and community council, as well as proactive usage of the media.

The School Setting

Newfield School is nestled within a quiet residential area, yet is close to the major interstate highway. Local residents hang around the corner convenience store two blocks from the school. The school is across from St. Mark's Church, which has a day-care program for the working parents in the neighborhood. The school is a small, three-story brick building reminiscent of turn-of-the-century architecture. Entrance into the building requires being buzzed in by the secretary, who monitors visitors via an outside camera, a procedure typical of many American schools today. Once inside the building, a visitor is immediately struck by a sense of warmth, comfort, and family. The old building has buffed and shiny hardwood floors and large classrooms with tall windows. The building is in need of many repairs in terms of painting, flooring, and windows, not to mention desks, chairs, rugs, and appropriate supplies. Many of these needs are being attended to due to the relentless efforts of the principal. She stops at nothing to improve the building, including paying for many things out of her own pocket. Despite needs, there is a sense of happiness and peace, with children actively learning as demonstrated by their attention and engagement. The hallways are filled with student work, awards, and other honors bestowed upon the school. The classrooms are colorful and homey.

Entering the building, a visitor climbs up three steps to the preschool room, kindergarten, and one special education classroom on the first floor. An enormous aquarium complete with colorful fish and plants adorns the center of the wall and adds to the sense of calm and peacefulness. The secretary and the principal are located on the second floor of the building, with their offices down the hall from one another. Signs guide visitors to the second-floor offices. The secretary greets everyone warmly in the office that is seldom quiet. At any given time, students, staff, parents, or visitors may be coming in and out of the office for a variety of reasons. Many times, the principal herself may be in the office tending to the needs of an individual; at other times, she sits behind the desk and answers the phone while the secretary handles other urgent matters.

MEET THE PRINCIPAL: CARMEN PEREZ-DICKSON

The principal of Newfield School, Carmen Perez-Dickson, is an energetic, committed, collaborative, servant-leader who is neither quiet nor shy. Although short in stature, she is an imposing woman whose presence is clearly known. She wears colorful clothing with matching jewelry. Her hair is short, cropped to her head, and auburn in color. Her eyes sparkle with enthusiasm and she radiates warmth and sincerity. Carmen loves to talk about her Newfield angels, her exceptional staff, and parents. She is delighted to share her school with anyone who wishes to visit. She also shared with me stories about her family background and childhood.

Carmen is the sixth child in a family of seven, the first child to be born in the United States. Her father emigrated from Puerto Rico and worked for four years traveling back and forth to visit his wife and children until he was established and able to move his family to mainland United States. A carpenter, he settled his family in Milford, Connecticut, and rented a small, two-bedroom house where Carmen was born. After a short time in Milford, the Perez family moved to Newfield Avenue in Bridgeport, a short distance from Newfield School. They lived in a three-bedroom apartment above a barbershop. Because the owners of the apartment did not want Carmen and her siblings to play in the yard, her father moved the family to a housing project in Bridgeport where they lived until 1969 when he purchased his own land and built his own house.

Throughout her life, Carmen's parents have been her inspiration. In the 1950s, there were not as many Hispanics in Connecticut as there are today. Other Hispanics who came would "look for my father and he would help them find homes, jobs, and medical assistance. He would always help and I remember as a small child people would come and stay at our house." Although small, Carmen's home was the "transition place" and was always open to others. Carmen does not know how her parents did everything they did. Only her father worked, they were considered poor, and yet there was always food for everybody. Her siblings would bring their friends home and her mother would feed everyone. "I never heard anyone not get invited to or even coerced by my mom to have dinner." To this day, Carmen still comes into contact with people who say "your mother made the best rice and beans." Carmen doesn't understand how her parents managed on her father's salary, but as she said, "I guess when you have a good spirit, God helps you."

3.1.   Carmen Perez-Dickson turns from the computer, pictured in a rare quiet moment in her office.

Carmen learned both Spanish and English when she was growing up. As a young child, she felt important when she would accompany her parents' friends to the hospital, store, or electric company to translate because they could not speak English. Her father would always volunteer her services as a translator. They did not have "tons of clothes like children do today" but enough so that if a child came over who needed a sweater, for example, her mother would give the child one of Carmen's or her sisters'. Carmen said that recycling items and just trying to help make life easier for others were lessons she learned from her parents. As Carmen said, "I saw the good they did and it just stayed in me and I always wanted to be that kind of person." Due to her parents' influence and inspiration, Carmen still gives away clothes and other things. She has created a clothing-recycling program in her school premised on a belief "that we all coexist and if we can help each other we do." Carmen and her children help with community dinners at Golden Hill Methodist Church on the last Wednesday of every month. She cooks and serves meals to the homeless and her children collect toys to bring to the homeless children. As she said, "It is just wanting to help, to make life easier for others."

Carmen went through the Bridgeport public schools and graduated from Warren Harding High School, where she was class president and prom queen. Because her parents were "strict Puerto Rican parents," they did not allow her to date and her brother took her to the prom. She was just happy to be there. Since she was not allowed to date, Carmen spent her leisure time reading. She began working every summer at the age of thirteen by tutoring other children.

Carmen's mother passed away three years ago, but her father passed away when she was sixteen years old. She remembered that day vividly. She was in typing class wearing an orange sweater and her teacher who called her the "sweater girl" had to give her the news. "Even though my father passed away in 1972, till this day he is the biggest influence in my life." She was honored to be with him and felt special when he chose her to go places with him. Carmen said her father told her to get a good education so that no matter what life dealt her she could always be independent and able to make it on her own. As a divorced mother of two, she said that because of her father's wisdom she has been making it on her own and "with God's blessing."

When she received a four-year academic scholarship to Connecticut College, Carmen went away from home for the first time, intending to be a translator. She had a triple major in Hispanic studies, education, and English. She graduated in 1978 and started working as a Spanish teacher at Foran High School, in Milford, Connecticut. Carmen taught at Foran for eleven years, sponsoring trips abroad with her students, many of whom are still in touch with her. Then she obtained a master's degree from Fairfield University in special education and bilingual education. Having a degree in special education has given Carmen the ability to look beyond a child's unruliness and to seek reasons for the behavior, a perspective that has enabled her to help students, parents, and faculty. Carmen completed her sixth-year professional diploma in educational leadership at Southern Connecticut State University and is currently a doctoral student in educational leadership at the same university. Carmen married in 1987 and gave birth to her son, José, in 1988 and her daughter, Luisa, in 1989. A divorced single mother since 1992, Carmen spoke with tremendous love and devotion about her children. She has strict restrictions and rules for her children but there is constant communication between them. Carmen and her children travel many places together and clearly there is a strong bond. The love she gives to her own children she also gives to her children at Newfield School, saying, "They are my Newfield angels."

Carmen has been an administrator in the Bridgeport public schools for over twelve years, with Newfield School her fourth school. Carmen lives in the city of Bridgeport and is very familiar with the issues that surround children of poverty. Carmen and her staff firmly believe that children are children and being poor is not an issue. They believe that all children can learn. Carmen communicates clearly that everyone in her school must do all that is possible to educate every child in the school. Carmen also goes beyond academics: it is her mission to make the lives of these children better. Developing character and self-esteem are equally important to academics in Newfield's curriculum. She gave examples in these words:

> We motivate everybody, we give attendance awards daily, we announce any kind of recognition, even teachers, on the intercom. Everything gets praised, and we give very clear expectations of what we expect children and teachers to do. We emphasize the Pillars of Character so the children know what kind of behavior is expected and we are fair and the children know what to expect. They know the rules and that there are consequences but as long as they are trying to follow expectations they are ok. We must all make the effort to strive to be successful. I think the clear expectations and that we know they are smart and they can do the work is important. We have high expectations and high standards and we will help our children achieve their potential. Then we kick it up a notch and see if we can get more. We are always *reaching for the stars*.

LEADERSHIP BY EXAMPLE

Carmen lives her word. She models what she says. This is clearly demonstrated by the many things that Carmen does for her students, staff, and parents. She models her belief that everything is her job. For example, she runs a food bank in her school where parents can come to get needed food supplies that they may not be able to purchase. She also has a clothing-recycling closet where anyone from staff to parents to community members can leave clothes that they no longer need so that other parents can come and select items needed for their children. The only requirement is that the clothes are cleaned first. Obviously, these practices are rooted in the strong beliefs that Carmen's parents instilled in her. Carmen will give a parent a ride to a job or an appointment if that is what is needed. She works tirelessly to empower everyone. As she said, "Empower the students so they can be productive, empower the parents so they can help themselves, empower the community. You have to lift the self-esteem, which is important in this city. It is important they know they are valued members of society."

The only way to summarize the many things that go on at Newfield School is to use Carmen's words. When asked specifically what they do at Newfield School to be so effective with high-poverty children and their families, Carmen had many examples like the following:

> We reach out. We have a lot of motivational meetings for our students and our parents too. We hold monthly meetings for our parents. A lot of our parents need parenting meetings, so we meet and teach them how to boost their child's self-confidence and help them with homework, how to hold a parent-teacher conference. Some parents are intimidated and we let them know whatever they ask is ok because you know your child better than we do. We talk to the parents about good touch–bad touch. We hold parent training.

Carmen also explained:

> I am always walking around; I am in every class twice a day. The teachers like it. They know that I am not spying on them. If they need anything, I get it; if their class is doing a special project, I go in and sit down. I validate what they do. We are in the community. This summer, we along with the community center did grassroots tennis. We have an after-school program that goes from 3 to 5 P.M. and we changed providers to St. Mark's Church that is right next door. This is really good because some of the parishioners come here to read aloud to the students. There is a partnership. St. Mark's also has a day care across the street and we have a pre-K so they will bring them over in the morning, pick them up at 11 and come back with the afternoon pre-K. This helps the parents because they can drop their child at 7:00 A.M. at St. Mark's, St. Mark's brings them here to school and picks them up, and they keep them till 7:00 P.M. when the parents get out of work.

3.2. Carmen frequently helps individual students during her daily visits to the class-rooms of Newfield School.

She talked about the importance of community partnerships with two examples:

> We have a partnership with ABC of Bridgeport who gave us thirty turkey baskets last year and I delivered them to the parents. Since some do not have cars or are handicapped, the janitor and I went to twenty out of the thirty homes and we delivered. My parents are not embarrassed to ask for anything. I consider it a godly honor that they come to me, that they are not embarrassed. We all have different needs and I feel very happy that my parents can come to me. Also, I joined the Lions Club and have been the Sight Saver director for two years. I send out the applications, review them for accuracy, and fax them to an optical company for kids and adults who need glasses, but don't have the insurance, or their insurance only covers one pair and they break. I get them free eyeglasses. We have lots of children who come here and need eyeglasses.

Finally, she expressed justifiable pride about an award won by the school:

> We just won the independent reading award, this little school for being the best in the district in reading, because we care. People say parents don't care

but that is not true; they do not give them what they need, like parenting classes, things that are basic to their survival. We like our job and it shows. We do not look down on anyone, we are not afraid of touching our parents and having them hug us. We're not phony. That does not work, just teaching to the test does not work. It has to be holistic. It has to be more than passing the test. We care about learning about others; we want our children to be sensitive to each other. We care about the whole child and family. We are a whole learning community.

The best way to sum up Carmen's leadership is through a story of an actual event that occurred. Around February of 2002, while making one of my many visits to Newfield School, Carmen told me a story about two young boys in her school. These two boys, ages five and six, are brothers who enrolled at Newfield School sometime around the end of November. On this particular Monday in February, Carmen waited till 6:30 P.M. for these two boys to be picked up from school. Finally, Carmen decided, as she has done on many occasions, to drive the boys home. She told me that as she approached the house, "it was completely dark and seemed scary." She did not receive a response as she continuously rang the doorbell so she left a note with her phone number on it and took the boys to her own home.

Carmen told me that around 11 P.M., after the boys were asleep, her phone rang and some unidentified person said he would come to pick up the children. Carmen asked where their mother was and she was informed that the mother was in New Orleans at Mardi Gras. Since this person was not an approved guardian, Carmen told him that she would bring the boys to school with her the next day. On Tuesday, once at school, Carmen finally got in contact with a neighbor of the children who confirmed that the mother was away and that she had left some teenagers at the house to take care of the boys. Carmen realized this was not safe and proceeded to track down the mother in New Orleans. As Carmen said, "I did not want to call DCF (Department of Children and Family Services) because taking these children away and putting them in the foster system was not the answer." Carmen wanted to work with this mother. She was able to contact the woman, who cried on the phone and begged Carmen not to call DCF. She said that she would find someone to take care of the boys until her return on Friday. Carmen questioned the responsibility level of anyone the mother would get to care for the boys and then told the mother to have someone bring the boys' pajamas, clothes, and toothbrushes and that she would take care of them until her return. However, Carmen made the mother promise to meet with her immediately upon her arrival.

Carmen proceeded to tell me how she took these boys home for four more nights, fed them, bathed them, played games with them and her own children, and gave them a secure and safe place to sleep. Carmen said that she noticed how thin these boys were. When they got diarrhea from eating a healthy meal, she knew that there was a malnutrition issue here and had the school nurse take the necessary steps to have the boys examined. When the mother returned, Carmen made it clear to her that if she did not see an improvement in the health of the two boys and in their eating habits, and if she took off again leaving an irresponsible person in charge, she would call DCF.

I sat there in amazement as Carmen relayed this to me. She told me, "They are manageable right now and can be helped, and we have to get these boys and their mother on the right track now." She is committed to this. Carmen felt that turning these boys over to DCF without making every attempt to help them and their mother would not be in the best interest of these children. When I commented on how incredible she was, she just looked at me and shrugged. She honestly did not think this was a big deal. After all, this is something she would do again and again, anything for the children, anything to get them the fundamentals they needed so they could be successful in school. This is leadership, this is heart, and this is being a servant to the community. In addition, the two boys have selected and been allowed to spend holidays and some weekends at Carmen's house. "My children love the boys as much as the boys love them. They have become part of my real family. It is funny because sometimes the boys bring their cousins too. So we have a day care going on in the backyard."

LEADERSHIP PATTERNS AND PRACTICES

Carmen epitomizes effective leadership. She clearly sees her position as a tool for empowering others and serving her students and staff. Carmen understands that the role of principal does not necessarily constitute leadership; it is how you lead and how self-aware you are. When asked, Carmen passionately described her leadership:

I lead with my heart, I love kids, I love my job. I want to empower them so they will be successful citizens in life and give them whatever foundations they will need, not only academic but how to deal socially. With the parents it is the same; they trust me. I am very approachable. I see myself as a facilitator, not only for the kids but the parents and the teachers. If I can't help them with their problems, I will look for a way to help them. Even with personal problems, my staff can come in and close the door. I give them a tissue and they can bare all. I treat them the way I would want to be dealt with. I deal with the school the way I would want my children dealt with. My leadership style? I am a hands-on person, I am involved in everything. I believe as a principal that everything is my job—social worker, psychologist. . . .

Interviews with staff and parents, as well as my own observations, focused on leadership. I visited Newfield School on a regular basis for an entire academic year. I interviewed the principal, all full-time faculty (total of thirteen), all paraprofessionals, specialists, and the homeschool coordinator (total of seven). I also interviewed three cafeteria workers and six parents. The total number of interviewees was thirty. All interviews were tape-recorded and then transcribed. I did classroom observations and made field notes, which were analyzed against the interview transcripts. The results from the interviews were analyzed according to groups (e.g., kindergarten teachers, first grade teachers). The interviews were analyzed for themes and supporting quotations were extracted from the transcripts. I began each interview with a general question seeking an overall sense of Newfield School.

Three major themes to describe Newfield School arose from the responses to the question "Tell me about Newfield School." The first theme was that the school has a "caring family environment." Comments supporting this theme included statements such as "It's home here, I don't feel like I am coming to work, but to my home," "It is a family, no one is afraid," and "The school works because we care, we are a family." Teachers, staff, and parents supported the theme further by stating that Perez-Dickson fostered this "caring family environment."

The second theme that describes the school was a "collaborative and collegial environment." Comments endlessly supported this theme. Teachers and staff remarked on how everyone in the school works together, all work is done collaboratively, and everyone is collegial. Teachers and staff

Table 3.1.   Summary of Themes in Responses to "Tell Me about Newfield School"

Response Frequency*	Themes in Interview Responses
30	Newfield School has a family environment.
26	Newfield School has a collaborative and collegial environment.
25	The principal is a supportive leader.

*N = 30

stated that Perez-Dickson is very collaborative and collegial and again fosters this in Newfield School.

A third theme that arose was "supportive leadership is the foundation." All of the interviewees made comments that the foundation of the school and its family-like environment was the supportive leadership style of Perez-Dickson. Any home needs a solid foundation made of mortar and bricks that will last a lifetime. The mortar and bricks of Newfield School is the "supportive leadership style" of Perez-Dickson. Comments taken from the interviews support this: "She is supportive of everyone and is always on top of things, she gets things done," "She really understands teachers and how children learn, she has a feeling for people, so she supports us in every way." Table 3.1 summarizes these three themes.

The Faculty and Staff Speak

Every teacher, paraprofessional, and staff member spoken to and interviewed conveyed enthusiasm, dedication, and a joy for being and working at Newfield School. The teachers' classrooms were welcoming, inviting, child centered, and bustling with activity. Teachers and staff members had stories to tell and were willing and excited to tell the story of Newfield School. The teachers and paraprofessionals varied in age and experience. Some were new to the school and others had been there for several years. Many had taught in other schools within the Bridgeport Public Schools and a couple of teachers had taught in other school districts within the state of Connecticut.

One teacher taught in a more-affluent town in Connecticut and came to Newfield School to be part of this incredible environment. Each and every interview and discussion with all of the teachers, paraprofessionals, and staff at Newfield School validated the theme of the school's leadership as the foundation of its success. Embedded within this was the strong sense of family and the collaboration and dedication among the administrator, faculty, staff, and parents. Several of the faculty and staff believed that the small size of the school helped to foster these attributes.

Every teacher and staff member indicated that it was the effective leadership that formed the foundation for Newfield's success. It was clearly stated that the sense of family, collaboration, and dedication could not exist without a strong, caring, and passionate leader. An interview question posed to the teachers and staff was: "Describe the leadership at Newfield School." Five themes emerged from analysis of the rich and inspiring responses and stories:

- She is supportive, caring, and creates a family.
- She is a dedicated and passionate role model.
- She is strong and sets high expectations.
- She is visible.
- She is a doer who gets things done.

(She is supportive, caring, and creates a family.)

Carmen's strong sense of family translates from her own home to Newfield School. She firmly believes that children should be treated the way she would want to have her own children treated. "She is family oriented and 100 percent for the kids." This sense of family is evident as one walks through Newfield School. You feel as though you have entered the living room of someone's warm and caring home. Carmen fosters communication between and among her faculty. As I walked through the hallways, I saw teachers, staff, volunteers, and parents discussing a myriad of topics related to the school and children. This has translated to the students; the children are delighted to be in school and willing to share their day with any visitor who arrives. All of the students are the responsibility of all of the faculty and staff. It is clear to anyone who enters the building that Newfield School is not just an organization or institution centered on learning but it is a family, a community. For Carmen, school is family — and that is the message she clearly sends. "It's home here, it's an extensive family that is incorporated here. I will be honest with you, when I am coming to work I never look at it as work, I absolutely love what I do every day that I am here. I am having a great time, it is family oriented."

Carmen grew up in a home where all were welcome and that is the same environment she has created at every school she has led. As one teacher poignantly put it, "It is like a family, no one is afraid. If they see another child in another classroom doing something, it doesn't matter if you are their teacher or not, the teachers around here will correct the child, so they know that everyone expects them to behave a certain way." Carmen expects nothing less. "I treat children the way I want my own child to be treated and I expect everyone else to do the same." This commitment has been made clear to all who are involved with Newfield School. Teachers, staff, and parents comment that the school is a family and that anyone can talk to anyone at any time. Newfield School epitomizes a kind, generous, and sharing environment. Operating as a family fosters everyone's commitment, dedication, and collaboration. Staff and teacher comments included these: "It's a family, easygoing; you are not pressured so I feel relaxed, happy to be here." "What makes it work? It is a family school; we're all a family. I love it, I love working here, it's a community-based school so I get to meet many of the parents, grandparents, family, and guardians. . . . I just like it here, I just keep saying the same thing over and over again, it's just like a family."

She is a dedicated and passionate role model.

Synonyms for dedication include devotion, commitment, enthusiasm, allegiance, and loyalty. Any of these words accurately describes Carmen, faculty, staff, and parents at Newfield School. Carmen was inspired by her parents to give to others; her parents' dedication to their community became ingrained in Carmen. This sense of duty is contagious in Newfield School. Teachers, specialists, paraprofessionals, and staff work as a devoted team who are committed to all of the students at Newfield School. There is a mutual respect that permeates the climate of Newfield School; there is no feeling that one adult is better than the next, only the commitment to do what is best for the children. Everyone is involved, including the cafeteria workers, custodian, and secretary. Carmen continually models collaboration. There are many synonyms to define the word *collaboration*: teamwork, partnership, group effort, relationship, and cooperation. As the teachers indicated, "She is not about authority, she is about helping us." They care for each student as if the child were their own; Carmen would not have it any other way. If a child needs to eat, the child is fed. If a child needs clothes, a child receives clothes. If a child needs eyeglasses, a child receives eyeglasses. Additionally, the school is kept clean and orderly so that the students have an environment that represents a home away from home.

The commitment to work collaboratively with full dedication to the students at Newfield School adds to the formula of success that they have. The faculty and staff themselves discuss this collaboration and dedication. "The students see how the staff interacts here, the kids see that Ms. B and Ms. S respect each other. . . . I think that it gives them a reason to strive to do their best. . . . When you come together with different perspectives, different experiences, different talents, and bringing it together collaboratively, the kids benefit from this," said a special ed teacher. A first grade teacher expressed her thoughts in these words:

> I will tell you that these teachers are dedicated. I was at another school yesterday and watched a social studies class. I am not saying that the teacher wasn't dedicated but the energy and enthusiasm wasn't there and I felt so bad for the students. . . . Our teachers are dedicated to their jobs. I mean if Ms. Dickson needs us to stay till 6:30 or 7:00 on a given night, I guarantee you'll find if not 100 percent, 99 percent of the teachers will be here. It's dedication, we are all dedicated.

Finally, a pre-K teacher said:

> It's the dedication. For example, if you go to a faculty room in most schools, the second they get into the faculty room they start complaining about administration, the kids, what they wanted and couldn't get; yet in our faculty room we are laughing and joking enjoying a few minutes of adult conversation and it is very healthy. We talk about home, current events, everything. We always talk at a professional level, we don't talk down to each other.

The teachers and staff feel a sense of ease and comfort with one another. They continually state how well they all get along, and it is obvious. Stop by the faculty lounge and you will hear them talking and laughing, sharing personal stories as well as success stories related to the students. Any discussion regarding a student who needs help has an optimistic and upbeat tone. They feel comfortable seeking each other out for advice and are supportive of each other's endeavors. They are supportive of one another, outgoing, and friendly—but then again, Carmen is the leader of "upbeat and friendly." "We get along fantastically, we work together, have lunch together . . . everyone is committed. As far as the staff is concerned, I have to be honest with you, we work together as one. We know all the kids." Time and time again, there were many references to the dedication of the staff members and their willingness to work so closely with the parents. It was evident that the parents, faculty, staff, and leader all worked together for the betterment of each and every child in Newfield School.

Newfield School is small in size in comparison to the average size of elementary schools within the United States. It is also a pre-K–3 elementary school, which adds to the small-size factor. Several of the teachers and staff stated that the small size enabled them to have a stronger sense of family and collaboration. However, when asked if the "magic" of Newfield School could be replicated in other schools that were larger in size, the response was always a unanimous "Yes, if you have leadership like Carmen's." Even though the teachers and staff described the smallness of the school as part of the reason for its success, it was obvious that the

3.3.   In a typical classroom moment, a second grade teacher engages three students in hands-on learning.

foundation of Newfield's success was and is anchored in effective leadership. "The key," said one teacher, "regardless of size, is to have an administrator who is visible, works with you, builds collaboration, and is passionate about children." Carmen is passionate about children. These are "her kids," "her Newfield angels."

She is strong and sets high expectations.

Carmen does what she has to do to make her school a success. Not even Central Office administration stops her. If she cannot get the resources or support she needs from Central Office, she seeks other ways and means to get what she needs for her school. As she said, "I have contacts in the community; if I need things, I ask for them. I write grants, I get the money, even if I have to use my own. I don't wait for downtown to give me the resources, I go after them on my own." Carmen encourages her staff to write grants. I dubbed her the "grant queen" and felt I could learn a thing or two from her. She has written grants to get *Scholastic News* for her students, to get eyeglasses, to get extra books, to have presenters come in, and even writes grants to get staff development for her teachers, staff, and parents. Every time I spoke to her, she was writing another grant. She has trained her teachers to write grants and encourages them to do so. She helps them with every detail and now the teachers initiate their own grants. I was amazed at how much Carmen and her faculty and staff members are able to achieve through this process and their high expectations. Carmen is relentless. She is passionate about her school. The words *passionate*, along with *caring*, *strong*, *supportive*, and *family oriented*, were used many times by faculty and staff to describe Carmen. These qualities are infectious and permeate throughout the school among all faculty and staff.

She is visible.

Carmen was clearly viewed as a visible leader, someone who was available to everyone including the students and parents. A kindergarten teacher said, "Her leadership is fantastic. She is on everything, she covers from A to Z on a daily basis. She is on top of everything; she is upfront and lets you know what is up. She is a role model." She clearly exhibits effective interpersonal skills and an ability to understand the needs of people. The childhood influences of making other people's lives better is apparent. It is Carmen's mantra.

Carmen is about leadership, not merely management. Teachers remarked how Carmen visits every classroom every day and talks to the students. "She knows what is going on in her building, she is always there, she is visible, and she is supportive." Said a first grade teacher:

> She is a principal but she is also a teacher and she really understands how people learn, how children learn. She has a feeling for people and that makes the difference. She is not so caught up in the politics . . . she really gets down to the meat of it. . . . Leadership is the major factor in making it happen. If the leader is just talking and not doing what they say, people can see right through that . . . she is right with us and she doesn't pretend to be with us; she is seriously with us.

Carmen knows the meaning of being collegial, cooperative, and a team player. These are things she learned from her parents, during the days when her father would have her translate for their Hispanic neighbors and friends. She learned the importance of being supportive and therefore she supports the teachers, staff, and students. Some teachers commented on the fact that in other schools they had taught in, this was not the case. "She knows the kids, she comes into the room; the other school I was in was very large. I never saw the principal, never was able to sit down and talk to her for anything." Carmen sees it a bit differently. "It is my job and it should be every principal's job. Size is not an excuse, you just have to be more creative." Carmen has worked at larger schools and a few teachers who worked with her previously followed her to Newfield School. Carmen's style of leadership has never wavered. Carmen is visible and approachable, and works side by side with her teachers and parents. She works in the after-school program and makes sure that the teachers have what they need to do the job. However, she expects the job to be done.

She is a doer who gets things done.

They described Carmen as a "doer," a very approachable leader who did not view her leadership as a role but rather a collaborative relationship with all staff, parents, and children to fulfill the mission of Newfield School. Teachers and staff highlighted all the work that Carmen does and how comfortable they felt in going to her for any concern. Their statements regarding Carmen's leadership encapsulate their feelings best. One first grade teacher said:

> She is human. . . . These kids know that she is not just an administrator, you know she is their friend, she is their mother, nurse. . . . It's not like "I am the principal, you are the teacher and you do as I say," it's "We are in this together, your opinions matter, I want your feedback," and she collaborates with us on everything. She is very supportive. For example, if you are writing a mini-grant and you win, you are awarded the money and they have a ceremony for you. She is going to be there.

A second grade teacher expressed her thoughts in these words:

> She couldn't be a better leader. . . . She is very relaxed and you don't get stressed. . . . I don't have any issues hanging over my head, they are addressed immediately. She is always open to our ideas regarding policy. We can talk to her about anything whether it's a broken pencil sharpener to "I think this child is dyslexic" . . . and she will *never* say, "I don't have time right now"—never. It's amazing.

Finally, a paraprofessional expressed a similar thought: "She gets things done right away. . . . She is a doer. She is very supportive to the staff, she always backs them up and is supportive of children and always makes them feel good. She is always there." Table 3.2 summarizes the five leadership themes that emerged from the faculty and staff interview responses.

Table 3.2.   Summary of Themes in Responses to "Describe the Leadership at Newfield School"

Response Frequency*	Themes in Interview Responses
20	She is supportive, caring, and creates a family.
18	She is a dedicated and passionate role model.
17	She is strong and sets high expectations.
17	She is visible.
16	She is a doer who gets things done.

*N = 20

The Parents Speak

Every parent spoken with had positive things to say about Newfield School. The parents credited the success of the school to its leader and the family environment she had created that empowered all faculty, staff, and parents. For example, one parent of a first grader said, "I love it here; personally, this is the best school because the principal is hands-on, it is so family based. The teachers are awesome. I love it here for my son, it is a challenge and I like the way they teach. In all the classrooms, parents are allowed to come in and watch what the teachers are doing. Open door policy, the teachers are approachable." Carmen has created a family atmosphere where the education and nurturance of the children come first. Her commitment to each and every student propels her to create an interactive relationship with the parents.

I was invited to attend an evening event where the parents were meeting to work on being part of a leadership council, a district goal set up by the superintendent. Carmen formed an advisory council that included parents when she arrived at Newfield School and among the topics of discussion was leadership. Carmen told me that there would be dinner prior to the meeting. I arrived to discover that Carmen was first feeding the children of the parents who could not get baby-sitters; then had arranged for volunteers, including her own children, to take care of the children while the meeting was in progress. After the children ate, the parents sat down to eat and talk. Carmen introduced me and explained what I was doing at Newfield School. Then she went into the kitchen to help serve the food. I was swarmed with parents, clamoring to talk about Carmen and Newfield School. They clearly saw Carmen's leadership as the foundation for the success of the school. Like the faculty and staff, the parents used words such as *caring*, *passionate*, *strong*, and *family oriented* to describe Carmen's leadership qualities. For example, one parent said:

> I like that Ms. Dickson, the principal, knows every parent by name and she knows every child by name. They don't have to be in trouble to be known, that is a reason why I love her, I just love the principal. She rewards the children for doing good, she treats them like they are her own, she treats them with love. She shows so much love to these kids, she nurtures them. I have never seen a school like this one, honestly, it's awesome. I really love this school.

Equal praise described the faculty and staff as devoted, committed, and caring. For example, one parent said, "Here they praise the children, they tell them encouraging things, say things like 'You did great today.' They don't say you are not going good. They encourage and challenge them. It's an awesome school." The parents also expressed appreciation for the welcoming atmosphere in the school that embraced their support and assistance in the classrooms. They felt that this sent a strong message to the children. "The parents are involved and it is key for the kids to see their mom here, watching and working with the teachers." Another parent of a first grader said:

> It is a learning environment, nobody here is afraid to walk up to the principal and talk to her about whatever problem they may have. They are not afraid to walk up to a teacher and I think that is needed. The parents have to be part of the school, they have to reinforce when the teachers give them homework. My son went to kindergarten in another school in the neighborhood and every day the teacher would say that he is not up to level. It ended up that he was transferred here because of classroom size. At first I was against it, but once he came I said it was the best thing for him. For the first two weeks I would ask the kindergarten teacher here, how he was doing, is he on task, is he having problems with any area and finally she said, "Why do you keep asking me that?" I said because the kindergarten teacher in the other school told me he wasn't on task. She said, "I don't know where that came from because I talk to your son every day, he does all his work and he is fine."

Carmen believes that parents must be involved in their child's education but she also firmly believes that they have to be respected and given the support that they need. "If I have to make a home visit, I do. If I have to drive a parent to an appointment, I do, and I expect that they will make their child's education a priority." Every parent I encountered had nothing but high praise for Carmen and her remarkable staff.

An interview question asked of every parent was "Tell me about the relationships between the principal, staff, and parents." The two themes that permeated the answers to this question were "The relationships are similar to being a family" and "Strong leadership is the foundation." With regard to the first theme, "relationships are similar to being a family," parents commented that they felt comfortable at Newfield School; it was like coming

Table 3.3. Summary of Themes in Responses to "Tell Me about the Relationships between the Principal, Staff, and Students"

Response Frequency*	Themes in Interview Responses
6	The school is a family.
4	Strong leadership is the foundation.

*N = 6

home. One parent commented, "It works here because we are family. I can call a teacher at any time and they respond, they are available." Another parent commented, "They listen to your problems. It's like talking to my own mother or grandmother." Parents' comments and statements supported the second theme, "strong leadership is the foundation." Parents made statements such as, "The leadership is the major factor in what happens here. She believes in the students and leads with this belief." Another parent commented, "She is strong, a secure leader, and because of this believes that all kids can learn." Table 3.3 summarizes these parent themes.

Carmen has created in Newfield School a true, total, family-learning community. It was clear from every encounter that I had with the parents at Newfield School that they believed it was the best school with the best principal and the best teachers. The parents were comfortable in speaking up and actively involving themselves with the school. They reached out to other parents and encouraged those who were not as involved to become more involved. Carmen fosters a family climate. She sponsors programs for the parents to help them with parenting and understanding the educational needs of their children. She assists parents who need medical attention, food, clothing, or leads for jobs. As she said, "Whatever it takes, I do—because if the children do not come to school fed, clothed, and feeling that mommy and daddy will be there when they get home, then they are upset and anxious. You must take care of these things, it is part of the educational process."

REFLECTION

Newfield School works! Being at Newfield School was a delight and pleasure. Every time I went, I wanted to spend the entire day there and was torn between university commitments and the school's enthusiastic, caring, and high-learning environment. Although an outsider, I was immediately welcomed by the principal, teachers, staff, parents, and students. The environment is engaging and everyone is eager to share the wonderful work that occurs in this school. The children are learning, consistently having the highest test scores for K–3 in the district; parents are involved; all staff work collaboratively, including teachers, paraprofessionals, cafeteria workers, custodians, and the secretary. Newfield School's climate is permeated with dedication, commitment, and a sense of family. Carmen would not have it any other way. "I make my expectations clear, and the children come first." Everyone in the school works tirelessly to make sure that the students develop academically, socially, and emotionally.

If Newfield School is so successful, the question becomes: Why aren't other schools with high numbers of children living in poverty able to replicate the environment and success of Newfield School? Is more money the answer? According to Carmen, the answer is no. She believes that we need accountability. "Educators need to do the job that they get paid for." She believes the school is the weak link; although resources are important and needed, the issue is accountability. "We need people to do the job they are getting paid to do. We have some people who come to put in their time and collect their paycheck. That is horrible, horrible. The school is the weak link especially when you have people who come in, show videos all day, water down the curriculum, and no one holds them accountable."

When asked, "What do educators need to do to begin improving the success of children, especially those from high-poverty areas?" she responded:

> You have to have heart and you have to treat everyone the way you would want to be treated. You have to have high expectations and understand that these parents are giving their children the best they can. If it is not in your heart, don't go into education. If society does not make education a priority, our society will crumble. Across society, education has been dumbed down. We need to get serious about education.

Poverty is not an issue at Newfield School—at least, not educationally. Socioeconomic status is not the basis for the level of education that the students receive. Students are inspired to believe that they can achieve to the uppermost limits of their individual capabilities. This inspiration comes from a deeply held belief that all children can learn that is demonstrated in the attitudes of everyone in the school community. As Carmen stated, "There are preconceived notions about ethnic backgrounds, notions that if you live in Bridgeport, even if you are a doctor or lawyer, it is your ethnic background that determines how you are treated. We do not do that here at Newfield." According to Carmen and her staff at Newfield School, all children can learn.

The commitment to the belief that all children can learn means that the Newfield School community does all it can to assist those in a low socioeconomic situation. Staff and faculty of Newfield School go beyond the four walls of their school building to meet the needs of their students. Everyone is held accountable. The development of children who live in poverty may be threatened by a variety of factors, including but not limited to inadequate nutrition, substance abuse, environmental toxins, and inadequate day care. Newfield School has partnerships with various organizations to provide the essentials of food, clothing, and medical assistance required by children living in poverty. They work with St. Mark's Church situated across the street from the school to provide before- and after-school programs for their students. The staff and faculty provide parenting classes and any other workshops that may be helpful to the parents in raising and educating their children. The principal will exhaust all of her resources to provide any assistance that a parent may need, whether that is food, clothing, a ride to a doctor's appointment, or day care for nonschool-age children so the parent can work. She is supported completely by her faculty and staff in these endeavors. The parents feel respected and empowered.

Recognition exists at Newfield School of the importance of meeting the basic needs of the child in order to secure the child's academic success. Newfield School does whatever it takes. The proof of their success can be seen in standardized test scores, as well as in individual performance portfolios of student work. However, the greatest success of the school is witnessed by experiencing this caring learning environment. This is a school that does not subscribe to stereotypes regarding poverty or children living in urban areas. For them, all children and parents alike can achieve academically and be emotionally healthy. They strive for this through the leadership of one servant-leader, Carmen Perez-Dickson.

Chapter Four

Comparing Harrison and Newfield Schools: Best Leadership Practices

Central to the leadership successes of the two principals in our case studies are their strong relational leadership skills and their high expectations. Each principal has created a caring, family school where high achievement is expected. The high expectations reflect their beliefs in the capability and promise of the children. In a previous profile of a caring principal, Lyman wrote, "A leader grounded in caring enhances learning by honoring emotions and empowering teachers to change and grow; by contributing to safe and supportive environments for students, parents, and teachers; and by viewing everyone from a positive perspective" (2000, 149). From that positive perspective, caring leadership enhances learning, rebuilds community, and advances social justice. Dillard also emphasizes that a "tenet of effective leadership in diverse ethnic and cultural group settings holds that concern, care, and advocacy for the individual needs of students is critical" (1995, 559). Caring is always a personal path that involves values and a principal's way of being in relationships. Caring leadership makes a difference, particularly in high-poverty schools.

In this chapter, we present a comparative analysis of the leadership practices of Aurthur Perkins and Carmen Perez-Dickson, as well as the learning environments of Harrison and Newfield schools. Basic similarities and differences of the schools are developed first. Leadership patterns and practices of the principals are compared, followed by a compilation of insights from surveys completed by faculty and staff about best leadership practices in high-poverty schools. We also discuss faculty and staff insights about best teaching practices in high-poverty schools. In the concluding section of the chapter, we share six actual stories. These stories illustrate Noddings's

73

(1984) three components of caring and demonstrate the depth of caring that students and families experience in these exceptional, uniquely caring school communities.

COMPARING THE SCHOOLS

Both Harrison and Newfield are elementary schools located in urban cities—one in Peoria, Illinois, and the other in Bridgeport, Connecticut. Harrison and Newfield have high proportions of children who are classified as low income: 99.7 percent for Harrison and 86.5 percent for Newfield. The number of children from non-English-speaking homes is 3.3 percent for Harrison and 11.2 percent for Newfield. Both schools have a high percentage of minority students. Harrison's racial/ethnic demographics for students consist of 89.3 percent African American, 2.3 percent Hispanic, and 7.2 percent non-Hispanic white students compared with Newfield's percentages of 73.4 percent African American, 25 percent Hispanic, and 1.1 percent non-Hispanic white students.

With large numbers of poor and minority children, both Harrison and Newfield do exceptionally well academically. The state of Illinois has rigorous state curriculum standards that are measured by the Illinois Standards Achievement Test (ISAT). In 2001, test results indicated that 66 percent of the Harrison third graders met or exceeded state standards for math, 54 percent met or exceeded the state standards for reading, and 70 percent met or exceeded state standards for writing. Connecticut also has rigorous state curriculum standards measured by the Connecticut Mastery Test (CMT). The test is administered the first time at the beginning of fourth grade. For the 2001 school year, CMT scores indicated that children from Newfield School outperformed district scores. In math, 55.3 percent of the students achieved mastery compared to the district average of 53.4 percent; in reading, 54 percent achieved mastery as compared to the district average of 37.5 percent; and in writing, 69.8 percent achieved mastery as compared to the district average of 57.3 percent.

To summarize the basic similarities, both Harrison and Newfield have welcoming, caring environments and are receptive to visitors, whether they are parents or outsiders from the community. Bringing about student learning is the central focus of each school. These two schools are located in separate states, close to 1,100 miles away from each other, and yet they have similar mission statements. Both schools are committed to the development of the whole child and the creation of nurturing environments. Both schools' mission statements contain the same words for what students will become—"lifelong learners and productive citizens."

The major differences between Harrison and Newfield are size and location. Harrison is a pre-K–4 school with a total of 475 students (piloting a fifth-grade class during the time of this research) as compared to Newfield, a pre-K–3 school with a total of 188 students. Harrison has a total staff of sixty-nine compared to Newfield's total staff of twenty-six individuals, including the principals. Although both schools are located in urban cities, Harrison School is located on the grounds of a public housing project in one of the poorest, high-crime areas in Peoria. Children from the project and surrounding neighborhood attend Harrison. Newfield School, on the other hand, is located in a quiet residential area across the street from St. Mark's Church. It is, however, close to a major interstate highway as well as the Long Island Sound. All the children who attend Newfield live in the neighborhood and the majority of them walk to school. It was difficult to ascertain other major differences between Harrison and Newfield. They have more commonalities than differences. Both schools are successful learning communities, a success that is related to their two dynamic leaders. Table 4.1 presents a summary of major similarities and differences.

Table 4.1. Summary of Demographic Comparisons of Harrison and Newfield Schools

Categories	Harrison	Newfield
Location	Urban	Urban
Grade Levels	Pre-K–4 (Pilot 5th grade at time of research)	Pre-K–3
Size	475 students	188 students
Faculty/Staff Size*	69	26
Site	Center of housing project in high-poverty neighborhood	Residential neighborhood
Percentage of Poverty	99.7%	86.5%
Race/Ethnicity of Students		
African American	89.3%	73.4%
Hispanic	2.3%	25.0%
Non-Hispanic White	7.2%	1.1%

*Totals include principals

COMPARING LEADERSHIP PATTERNS
AND PRACTICES OF THE PRINCIPALS

The leadership patterns and practices of Aurthur Perkins and Carmen Perez-Dickson echo descriptions from other case studies of principals whose voices represent diverse perspectives (Ah Nee-Benham and Cooper 1998; Dillard 1995; Lomotey 1989; Murtadha-Watts 1999; Reyes, Scribner, and Scribner 1999; Scheurich 1998; Quint 1994). Reading their physical descriptions in chapters 2 and 3, readers might believe they were reading about the same individual. Both women are energetic and uplifting people who carry themselves with confidence. Perkins and Perez-Dickson are both minority women raised in urban cities. Perkins is African American and Perez-Dickson is Hispanic. Both have strong religious beliefs and their actions are guided by these values. Both hold graduate degrees and have strong commitments as professional educators to creating a school community of learners that is like a family.

Leadership Similarities

A strong leadership similarity is the supportive, relational approach each principal has taken to creating a school environment that operates and feels like a family. Both women value and treat their teachers, staff, parents, and children as family. Everyone has a stake in the education of each and every child. As Perez-Dickson stated, "I treat each child the way I would want my own child to be treated and I expect the same from everyone." She is firm about this. Perkins also expects no less, her values being tied (as are Perez-Dickson's) to strong religious and family values. In Perkins's words, "I want us to be a family, a happy family. I work very hard to promote that atmosphere." In both schools, the children's parents are regarded as equal members of the school family.

Both these principals have worked hard to ensure that parents are involved with the school and their children's education. Perkins and Perez-Dickson work tirelessly to build relationships with parents. They get parents involved in the school by creating various opportunities. For example, Perez-Dickson has a leadership committee of which parents are a part, she has parent volunteers in the school on a daily basis, and she will make home visits and drive parents to appointments, if necessary. She appreciates and respects parents and will do anything to get them to become involved and active participants in their children's education. Perkins also utilizes parent and community volunteers. She has facilitated the creation of a series of educational programs for parents, from GED programs to those focused on parenting skills. She makes impromptu home visits if a child is in trouble or she needs extra support or involvement from a parent. She routinely hires parents to serve as aides in the cafeteria and in the preschool programs. Her ability to communicate with parents is rooted in her own experiences with poverty and having a baby at age thirteen. She has walked in their shoes and she is a powerful exemplar of what is possible.

Researchers (Dauber and Epstein 1993; Mortimore, Sammons, Stoll, Lewis, and Ecob 1988; Schorr 1988) have stated that parent involvement leads to positive influences upon a student's progress and development. This involvement needs to go beyond helping with homework to include visits to the school, work in the classrooms, and attendance at meetings. Parents who participate in the school community send an important message to students that education is important. The research indicates that parents must be partners with educators and that such partnership is especially important for parents who are not well educated or sophisticated in dealing with schools. Both these women understand, value, and facilitate parent involvement. Their parents are active and valued partners in the school family.

In addition to having a strong relational approach that builds a family, an equally compelling leadership similarity is that each principal is respected for being a strong person who gets things done. Sometimes getting things done is a result of their own energetic efforts, yet each understands that more is accomplished through a team effort. Perkins and Perez-Dickson understand the importance of empowering their faculty and staff. They accomplish this by being supportive and encouraging of the endeavors that their faculty and staff wish to pursue. They facilitate creativity and innovation in their schools. However, both these women recognize that facilitating the leadership of others is "power sharing" and each remains clearly in charge (Fullan 1997). Each is a principal who supports and stimulates initiative while maintaining a clear focus and moral purpose that is rooted in strength (Fullan 1999, 2003). In describing both Perkins and Perez-Dickson, the words *supportive*, *giving*, *caring* yet *tough*, *strong*, and *direct* were repeatedly heard. Each principal's success illustrates the power of leadership practices that combine support with pressure (Fullan 1999; Sebring and Bryk 2000).

Riester, Pursch, and Skrla (2002) studied a mixed group of Texas principals of extremely successful high-poverty schools, four women and two men. Two were Hispanic, one African American, and three were white. The authors clustered the beliefs and practices of these principals into three major themes: "(1) promoting a democratic culture; (2) adopting a prescriptive approach to literacy and academic success; and (3) demonstrating a stubborn persistence in 'getting there'" (292). The democratic culture theme includes commitment to the success of all the children, "a teaching environment characterized by high levels of freedom and openness" (294), and empowerment of professional staff. Each of these components could also be used to frame the descriptions of Aurthur Perkins and Carmen Perez-Dickson.

Holding high expectations of themselves and all others involved in the school community is a third way that Perkins and Perez-Dickson are similar as leaders. Partly because of their personal backgrounds, both women have a clear vision regarding the needs of children their schools serve. Each wants a better future for the children. Barth states, "The moment of greatest learning for any of us is when we find ourselves responsible for a problem that we care desperately to resolve" (1990, 136). Sergiovanni (1984) describes the effective principal as an individual who is similar to a high priest, someone who leads others to have faith in enduring values, beliefs, and cultural strands that are the foundation and essence of a school's culture, climate, and identity. He is adamant about consistency of words and deeds, writing, "The leader stands for certain ideals and principles which become cornerstones of their very being." Perkins and Perez-Dickson clearly advocate their values and the belief that all children can learn, become lifelong learners and productive citizens, and that poverty may be a circumstance of their lives but is not the decisive factor in whether they will achieve. This vision has power because it has become the collective vision in each school community. Sergiovanni (1991) describes the role of collective vision to leadership in these words:

> Vision is an important dimension of purposing and without it the very point of leadership is missed, but the vision of the school must also reflect the hopes and dreams, the needs and interests, the values and beliefs of everyone who has a stake in the school—teachers, parents, and students. In the end, it is what the school stands for that counts . . . a binding and solemn agreement needs to emerge that represents a value system for living together and that provides the basis for decisions and actions. This binding and solemn agreement represents the school's covenant. When both vision and

covenant are present, teachers and students respond with increased motivation and commitment and their performance is beyond expectations. (135)

In summary, Perkins and Perez-Dickson are committed to the vision of
every child learning and achieving to his or her highest potential. Neither
the attitudes nor behaviors of either woman are rooted in deficit thinking regarding children's worth and potential, whatever their economic situation or
racial/ethnic heritage. Both women model a vision of success for all children by having the highest expectations for themselves and expecting nothing less from students or faculty and staff. Deficit thinking is simply not per-
mitted, a factor others have found central to leadership for learning and
achievement in high-poverty schools (Delpit 1995; Riester, Pursch, and
Skrla 2002; Scheurich 1998; Shields 2003; Wagstaff and Fusarelli 1995).

A fourth similarity in their leadership is the high energy and dedication
of each principal, considered role models by staff, parents, and the students.
Spiritual values play a central role in who each is as a person and leader.
Perkins and Perez-Dickson illustrate through their leadership what others
have written about the power of living your spiritual values. For example,
writing about other minority women leaders, Ah Nee-Benham and Cooper
(1998) share stories that exhibit determination and courage, as well as "a
sense of compassion toward all children and a determination to help children to learn, grow, and overcome whatever obstacles are placed in their
way. Their sense of equity and justice has been enhanced by their own experiences as minorities" (144). Scheurich speaks of the imperative for a
principal to act out of love if schools for high-poverty minority students are
to be transformed (1998, 470). Speaking of another principal, Quint shares
a teacher's description: "She fueled a sense of what was ethically right and
intrinsically wrong as she imbued each teacher with the values, beliefs, and
convictions that sustained her own perseverance and psychological
strength" (1994, 24). What Dillard writes of an African American high
school principal could be said of either Perkins or Perez-Dickson: "She nur-
tures—and leads—by her presence, by her example, by the way she con-
ducts her life and work in 'putting herself on the line for them'" (1995, 557).
Finally, Murtadha-Watts writes about how "African American women in
leadership positions often draw upon profound historical traditions of inner
spiritual strength as well as an activist ethic of risk/urgency" (1999,
155–56). She states that in her study of twenty-five African American

women in leadership roles, many "refer to spirituality as their source of strength and guidance" (156), as do Perkins and Perez-Dickson. They exemplify the power of leadership grounded in spiritual values.

A fifth leadership similarity is the above-and-beyond effort manifested in a variety of ways, including visibility. Each is described as a constant visible presence in the halls and classrooms of their schools, serving as role models and exemplars for the faculty and staff as well as the children. As Perez-Dickson's secretary stated, "You'll never find her in her office. She is in every classroom, in the hallways, cafeteria, playground—wherever the children are, that is where you will find her." Perkins begins her day in the gym greeting the children, handing out compliments, and reminding them of the rules of good behavior. She is often with the children on the playground at lunch. Her presence in and out of the office centers on actions and interactions with students, faculty, staff, and visitors. She is without equal in her ability to calm disturbed and angry students, investing much time in troubled students by taking a personal approach to correcting unacceptable behaviors. She arrives at Harrison early, and stays until the after-school activities have ended and the children have left the building. The dedication and above-and-beyond effort of each woman is recognized as exemplary.

As leaders, Perkins and Perez-Dickson have created caring, supportive communities in their schools, get things done, have high expectations, are role models, and give above-and-beyond effort. Emerging from faculty, staff, and parent responses to questions about leadership, these common themes in the leadership practices of Aurthur Perkins and Carmen Perez-Dickson are summarized in table 4.2.

Table 4.2.   Common Themes in Responses to Questions about the Leadership of Aurthur Perkins and Carmen Perez-Dickson

Leadership Themes of Perkins	Leadership Themes of Perez-Dickson
She takes a relational approach with staff and parents.	She is supportive, caring, and creates a family.
She is willing to take charge.	She is a doer who gets things done.
She has a clear vision and high expectations.	She is strong and sets high expectations.
She is an exemplar and role model.	She is a dedicated and passionate role model.
She gives above-and-beyond effort.	She is visible.

Additionally, they live their values, embody moral purpose, understand leadership as a collective enterprise, and have fundamentally shaped their schools. They exemplify the best leadership practices for high-poverty schools. They illustrate Fullan's (2003) understanding of what makes effective leadership in difficult situations possible. He writes: "The most important thing to know is that the combination of moral purpose and relational trust generates the wherewithal to go the extra mile. It makes a complex, difficult journey worthwhile and doable" (62).

Leadership Differences

The leadership differences between Perkins and Perez-Dickson are few. Their life experiences, although similar in some respects, took them down different avenues but led them both to the same place as educators and effective leaders. Although both women are minorities and were raised in urban cities, each had very different personal experiences. Perkins's father never lived in the home, while Perez-Dickson credits her father with being the major influence on her life. Perkins had her first child at age thirteen and dropped out of school, only returning because of outrage that African American children could not read. That experience while a volunteer in her children's school, coupled with a religious awakening, led her to go back to school and complete her education, finishing with a master's degree. A lifelong learner, the passion she felt to do something about the injustice being done to African American children set her on the path to the place where she is today. Perez-Dickson, on the other hand, grew up with both parents who guided her according to strict standards characteristic of their Puerto Rican heritage. She completed high school, went on to receive a four-year academic scholarship to Connecticut College, and obtained her master's degree and sixth-year professional diploma. A firm belief that by giving education to others she was giving them something that could not be taken away led her to the position she holds today as an educator and leader. Because of differences in personality and style, Perkins and Perez-Dickson may approach some things in their schools in a different manner but their beliefs and values are the same. Yes, they are different women—but they are the same in their strong conviction, passion, determination, and commitment to make a difference in the lives of children who come from poverty.

Discussion

Both Scheurich (1998) and Lomotey (1989) suggest that the most effective principals in high-poverty schools with large numbers of minority
children will be persons of color. For example, in concluding case studies
of three African American principals, Lomotey describes all three as having in common "a commitment to the education of African American children; a compassion for, and understanding of, their students and of the
communities in which they work; and a confidence in the ability of all
African American children to learn" (1989, 131). He argues that these
unique qualities of African American principals may "supersede all others
in importance in bringing about success" (131). In a later article reflecting on his previous work, Lomotey contended that African American
principals become more powerful as leaders when "they view their
African American culture as a significant bond with their students" (1993,
397). He refers to assuming this affinity as essential to taking what he
calls an ethno-humanist role as a principal. Lomotey writes, "The affinity
associated with this second role is facilitated, in part, by what political sci-
entists refer to as 'homophily'—the notion that people with homogeneous
beliefs, values, and cultural attributes tend to interact and communicate
more effectively with each other" (1993, 397).

Scheurich noted that the grassroots model developed in the successful
and loving schools he studied "arose principally from the loving and passionate commitment to the schools' children on the parts of the principals,
who in every case has been a person of color, although it also arose from
the commitments of the school staffs, who represent all races" (1998, 453).
He identifies the source of the model as communities of color, noting that
the "'love ethic' of HiPass schools is rooted in a historical communal practice of communities of color" (463). He elaborates with these words:

> It is as if in particular the principals (again, who all were persons of color)
> have a sense of historical solidarity or union with the children of color, so
> that the plight of the children is their plight, the needs of the children are
> their needs, and the successes of the children are their successes. . . . This
> lovingness is always there. It is pervasive, it inhabits everything they do or
> say. It also seems, to me, to be a source of endless energy to always do more
> for the children. (463–64)

Haberman (1999) presents a similar perspective, but does not connect potential for being a successful principal of a high-poverty school to a person's race. He does connect such potential with belief or ideology, writing:

> Individuals who already hold the ideology that characterizes star principals can benefit from subsequent training and learn the effective behaviors. For those who do not espouse the ideology, the behavioral training will result in a hollow and ritualistic performance without commitment and understanding. . . . The ideology is a value-laden system of beliefs caught and developed by life experiences rather than taught in graduate courses of school administration. (xi)

Our sense is that the leadership of Perkins and Perez-Dickson as principals is motivated by a love with deep religious and historical roots, a love that they extend to all children. They would agree that a degree of their success in connecting with the children and their families comes from personal experiences with the struggle to overcome poverty. They would also agree that the most successful leaders are those who believe in the worth and potential of minority children from low-income homes and that whatever their race or ethnicity, this belief is the key to any principal's success in high-poverty schools.

FACULTY AND STAFF INSIGHTS ABOUT BEST LEADERSHIP PRACTICES

Correspondences between how faculty and staff at the schools view best leadership practices and their two principals are striking. In written surveys given at both schools, faculty and staff were asked two questions relating to best practices of leadership and two questions about best practices of teaching in high-poverty schools. A total of thirty-six surveys were received, twenty-six from Harrison and ten from Newfield. The thoughtful and considered answers provide important insights and validate our observations. Two survey questions focused on what children living in poverty need from leaders, both principals and those in the central office. The two questions were:

(a) What do you think educational leaders can do for children who live in poverty?

(b) What central office/district practices support or impede the type of educational leadership needed to educate children of poverty?

Responses to the question about principals clustered in four categories.
The number one priority involved securing funding and other resources to
enhance teaching and learning. In the words of one respondent, "Make
sure the money is there to implement the programs and the materials
needed. Encourage people in the community to volunteer and to tutor children at school." Other suggested uses for such resources were recruiting
volunteers and appropriate numbers of staff, including specialized staff
and aides; having small classes; and providing teachers with training and
professional development so teachers would know how best to teach the
children. Associated with this priority were the following responses:
teaching the value of learning, going the extra mile to meet students'
needs, making school an on-task learning environment, developing programs for communication/language skills, and providing after-school
programs.

A second high-priority category was for leaders to be mentors and
role models for the children; to give love, support, and praise as well as
constructive criticism to the children; and to support their self-esteem.
One respondent wrote, "Connect with the students. Be a friend, leader,
and a mentor. Value your students' thoughts, feelings, and learning experiences." Another wrote poignantly, "Probably one of the best things
is to make them feel good about who they are. Our children need to learn
to like themselves. Many students have low self-esteem, are unhappy or
outright angry, and are not even sure why. These students need to feel
important, like they really do matter." Associated responses were the
following: to believe in the possibilities of and for the children and let
them know they matter; to give them a dream of who they can be and
how they can get out of poverty; to provide for basic needs of the students; to value students' thoughts, feelings, and learning experiences; to
teach and build respect; to keep expectations high; and to help them
reach their potential.

The third category was to provide opportunities for experiences to build
knowledge that is lacking, including field trips and before- and after-
school activities. Associated with this priority were the following
specifics: the desire for the principal to provide a positive, safe classroom

and school environment; programs targeted to students' needs; and educational opportunities that make sense to them and connect with their experiences. The final priority was to develop educational and parenting programs for parents; to educate parents through home visits; to connect with the students, their families, and teacher; and to communicate with the community. For example, one person wrote, "Develop the school as a community center with after-school programs for parents as well as children." Another wrote, "We need more educational programs for the parents. They have got to realize how important education is for their children and for themselves." Table 4.3 summarizes these categories of responses.

Survey respondents did not have as much to say about leadership needed from central office. That fact is a statement that speaks volumes. Some respondents offered no comments. No particular categories emerged. One respondent wrote, "Our school district is run by people who haven't experienced poverty or anything close to it. They seem reluctant to experience the true environment that children are expected to learn in. Why don't they set up their offices for a week in some of the schools?" One respondent asked for site-based decision making and two suggested a need for education of the attitudes of those in central office. Other suggestions were for central office administrators to reduce excessive assessment, allow for adaptation of districtwide curriculum standards, provide more funding, increase staff and reduce class size, provide recognition, and to get into high-poverty schools for extended periods of time in order to truly experience the environments and understand the needs of the schools.

Table 4.3. Summary of Themes in Responses to Survey Question "What Can Leaders Do for Students Living in Poverty?"

Themes* in Survey Responses**
1. Obtain funding and other resources to enhance teaching and learning.
2. Be a mentor and role model who gives love, constructive criticism, and emotional support.
3. Provide opportunities for experiences to build knowledge the students lack.
4. Connect strongly with parents through programs and relationships.

*Themes listed in order of frequency
**N = 36

FACULTY AND STAFF INSIGHTS
ABOUT BEST TEACHING PRACTICES

Faculty and staff responded to two written survey questions relating to best practices of teaching in high-poverty schools. The two questions about teaching were:

(a) What do you think educators need to do to assist children in poverty to succeed academically?
(b) What do you think are the best practices that can be developed for educating children in poverty?

Many who responded to the survey gave explicit and lengthy answers. All responses to both questions were analyzed for themes. Repetitions were collapsed into single categories and still the list contained forty-eight different suggestions. Further analysis, however, revealed that four themes were expressed with the greatest frequency, and emerged in answers to both of the questions.

The first of these major themes was the importance of knowing the children and understanding their home situations so that teaching can start from where they are. One respondent wrote, "First, know the child! This takes time and effort to know the child on a personal basis, but it's crucial for success. This relationship will allow both you and the student to discover what's needed for the child to succeed." Associated quotations were: "Take into consideration each student's situation individually"; "Show an understanding for what they may deal with outside of the school environment but teach them it cannot be an excuse"; "Build on prior knowledge"; and "Subject matter must be related to the students' experiences." One teacher wrote, "The 'best practices' for children in poverty are teaching them from where they are to start and then pushing them beyond what they ever imagined. It's easier said than done, but it can be done."

The second major theme was the importance of believing in the children's potential for success and supporting them in every possible way, including emotionally through hugs, encouragement, and love. Associated responses were the following quotations: "Educators need to have a mindset that these students can and will succeed no matter what"; "Believe in

them. Express love in words (e.g., I love you) and actions (e.g., hugs)";
"Educators need to show students that we believe in them. We need to be
supportive and let them know we want them to be successful"; "Educators
need to show that they care and expect every child to do their best and
meet their expectations to succeed academically"; "We need to be sure
that we let the children know how smart and bright they are"; and "Love
your students no matter what."

The third major theme consisted of descriptions of the types of instructional practices the respondents had found successful. Teachers' responses
were divided between those who found structured learning experiences
and approaches to be most successful and those who favored what they
called "hands-on exciting approaches" to learning. Teachers from both
camps emphasized high expectations. Responses associated with structured approaches were the following quotations: "Repetition, consistency,
lots of routines and procedures"; "Daily review of math facts and various
skills and concepts at each grade level"; "Explicit instruction in language,
phonemic awareness, phonics, sight words, and comprehension"; and
"Teach in a very organized and structured way." Other teachers, in contrast, emphasized the importance of hands-on learning, being willing to let
the children explore and discover, and creating exciting learning environments. Quotations from this perspective included "Provide hands-on exciting ways of teaching;" "These children need to be accelerated, not re-
mediated"; "Use lots and lots of hands-on learning that actively involves
the students"; and "Provide the best opportunities to discover and learn."

The fourth of these major themes was the importance of working with
the families in partnering and productive ways, providing them with resources and programs. Associated quotations were the following: "We
need to get the parents involved in the educational process"; "In order to
teach to the whole child, the school, the parent, and the child have to
work together to make a successful child"; "I think there needs to be a
good line of communication open with the parents"; and "We need to involve the whole family in programs and educate the parents too." Two
themes emerging with less frequency, but also noteworthy, addressed
teachers' expectations for themselves as professionals: being role models of good values and behaviors, and being willing to give the extra
time and effort required to help the children be successful. Examples included the teacher who wrote, "Educators need to love their jobs and

pass on a passion for learning, exploring, and discovering. They need to ensure an exciting resource-full learning environment"; "Be honest with them and promote values"; and "Educators need to be aware of the extra time that is necessary. Educators need to be prepared to go above and beyond."

STORIES OF CARING

The successes of Perkins and Perez-Dickson as principals emerge from the caring, supportive environments each has created. Importantly, the circle of caring in each school includes the families. Such caring environments are particularly important for the success of children in high-poverty schools. "Good principals model care. Their words and behavior explicitly show that caring is not optional. Nothing can substitute for this leadership" (Rooney 2003, 76). Good teachers also model care, as reflected in the words of a teacher interviewed at Harrison:

> We are working with children who need a strong consistent individual in their lives on a daily basis, someone who expects something from them but who does it in a caring way. I think I am a very compassionate teacher and I hope that the children see that. The only way I think our children respond to us is by knowing that "Yes, she is strict with me, but she also loves me." The children need to know by looking in my eyes that I do care about their success and that I do care about them as individuals.

Success stories shared by the teachers and staff members we interviewed demonstrate the power of caring to reach students and family members. Many educators think it is enough to have caring as a life purpose, value, or ethical orientation. Another approach to defining caring, however, is to understand it as a process or way of being in relationships (Noddings 1984). We use this meaning of caring as a way of being in relationships — with components of engrossment, action, and reciprocity — to anchor and organize stories of caring from our schools. Each person walks the path of caring differently, but unless caring moves into our way of being in relationships, how will others know that we care?

Engrossment

Noddings (1984) defines engrossment as being present in the acts of caring and focusing one's attention on the one cared-for. The concept also includes "regard, a desire for the other's well-being" (19). A story told by a first grade teacher illustrates this capacity to become engrossed in her student's reality. The story illustrates how children in high-poverty schools often live in confusing and contradictory realities. "Yesterday," the teacher said, "I helped a first grader lose his tooth. Then I tied it on a string around his neck and told him about putting it under his pillow, that the tooth fairy might come." She continued:

> He was a first grader who was pretty attached to me. He came back the next day and he still had the tooth around his neck. He said he told his family about why you put the tooth under your pillow, but the next morning it was still there so he decided to just wear it. He seemed more interested in showing me his uncle's name in the paper. So I got the paper, we found the name and sure enough, the uncle was in jail. He proceeded to tell me what he was in jail for in great detail. I just wanted to take him home with me. Sometimes the reality the children live with and share with you is so devastating that you can only listen. And I did, and we went on, and I let him feed the fish, and he seemed to totally forget about his uncle after that, seemed happy with the tooth on a string around his neck.

The story illustrates engrossment in the willingness of a teacher to engage with a little boy, to pay attention to him and help with his loose tooth, to hear all the details about his uncle, and finally—having taken in his reality—to let him feed the fish.

A second example of engrossment is about a speech and language pathologist who took a second look at a bizarrely behaving child who chewed on his clothes, and discovered a gifted kindergartner. The child came to her office to be reevaluated for speech at the request of his teacher, who believed that he should be classified as mentally handicapped. As he sat on the stool in her office, he fidgeted, scowled, and pulled the arm of his shirt way down over his hand. The sleeve was all wet, dirty, and chewed up. Something about him made her wonder if he had some sort of syndrome. "After years of working with children, you sometimes get this feeling just by looking at them," she said. So she tried to get a language sample, asking "What books do you like? What stories do you like?" He replied with a whole series of things like *Wild Wild Hair* and *Frog and Toad Go Shopping*. She noticed his eyes darting everywhere and suddenly realized that he was reading the titles of her books. So she got one of the books, gave it to him, and he read the whole thing. She asked him how he had learned to read, who had taught him, and his reply was, "Nobody, I taught myself." Subsequent tests showed no language impairment but his teacher still could not figure out what to do with him in the classroom. Speech and language pathologist Patricia Lindberg and Perkins decided to try putting him in a first grade room, that maybe if he were challenged the bizarre behavior and clothes chewing would stop. Essentially, along with provision for a one-on-one aide, this strategy worked. As a third grader, he is by and large a normal-acting child, a year ahead academically, and recommended for the gifted school. This story illustrates engrossment in the willingness of the speech pathologist to pay close attention to an odd little child who was doing weird things. She cared enough, had enough regard for the child, to look again and found not a mentally handicapped child but a socially delayed, gifted child who had taught himself to read in kindergarten.

Action

Noddings writes that action is "directed toward the welfare, protection, or enhancement of the cared-for" (1984, 23). A story told by a first-year teacher illustrates an action that enhanced a young girl's life. The teacher had worked hard all first semester with a very challenging girl who was twelve or thirteen in the fifth grade and in danger of failing again. The teacher tried everything she knew, including many conferences with the parent and the principal. Eventually, the girl understood that if she did not improve her work and behaviors she would fail again, and her behavior began to improve. By January, she was sometimes getting to stay after school in the classroom, a reward the teacher offered to well-behaved students, many of whom had no other place to go. One of those nights, the girl was still in the classroom when the teacher needed to leave for a church function, so she asked the student if she wanted to come along. The girl went and loved it so much the teacher started taking her to church with her on Wednesday nights whenever she had an A or B on the behavior chart for the whole week. This activity over the course of the second semester had a profound effect on the girl. Says her teacher, "I found a way to give her positive attention. It takes a lot of time but it is worth it to me to see her change so much. Her heart and attitude have changed. Now if they have turned in their homework and behaved, I take a bunch of my kids with me to church on Wednesday nights. They really enjoy getting to eat at my house beforehand." This story illustrates a whole series of caring actions by a beginning teacher.

A second story illustrating caring action is about the collaboration of a teacher who would not give up and a caseworker who filed a petition for educational neglect against a mother. The mother was the parent of five boys who were all chronically truant. The caseworker explained how, after months of his efforts, she had repeatedly "told me what I wanted to hear, but nothing changed." Finally he filed a petition for educational neglect and she made a complete turnaround—not overnight but over a period of a couple of years. A particularly caring teacher continued to work with the mother, insisting that she do what her children needed. She would not take no for an answer. Later the mother said to the teacher, "At one time I hated you, could not stand you, but I think a lot about you now and how you helped me by staying on me." Now the school district employs her as a cafeteria worker and her boys are on the honor roll. She and her husband have remodeled their house and are doing well. Although she no longer has children at this school, she maintains contact with the teacher and the caseworker who invested so much care in her. She calls or stops by periodically to share her progress with them and uses them both for sounding boards when she needs advice. This story illustrates that the actions of caring are often tough, that caring is not about being either a softy or a pushover.

Reciprocity

Reciprocity is the most complex component of Noddings's conception of caring and the one most often misunderstood by educators. Reciprocity requires an attitude of mutual respect and acceptance that facilitates a response or confirmation from the cared-for that caring has indeed occurred. Noddings writes, "As we examine what it means to care and be cared for, we shall see that both parties contribute to the relation; my caring must somehow be completed in the other if the relation is to be described as caring"

(1984, 38). This phenomenon of response she labels reciprocity. "The cared-for responds to the presence of the one caring," she explains (60). This response is facilitated by the "attitude of warm acceptance and trust [that] is important in all caring relationships" (65). The cafeteria manager told a haunting story that illustrates reciprocity. Worrying about and getting to know a little pre-K boy who would not eat, she discovered that his mother who was quite ill used to beat him. The cafeteria manager talked with him about how he needed to eat and would often have the child sit beside her. Frequently, she'd tear off or put in a bowl just a small amount of whatever was served for him, telling him that he would need to eat just that much in order to go outside. And he would eat just that much. After his mother died, he became a completely different child. He started to put on weight, she told me, and "will come down in the mornings if he is late and say, 'Miss Carol, can I have cereal instead of a donut?' I always say I don't care, and invite him to go help himself," she said. He knows he is at home here, and he walks in and gets what he wants and walks back out. He always says thank you on the way out. "I try to give them all that atmosphere of being at home here," she explained. The child's easy, at-home behavior shows that he feels accepted by the reciprocal attitude behind the care and love expressed consistently over time by the cafeteria manager.

A second story is about a mother who bought a teacher and her assistant gifts with money she had been given to spend on herself. She was the mother of a child in the pre-K program and was involved with a parent education program offered at the school. The teacher had worked with her over the years, having several of her children. They were always late to school and the mother had not been particularly cooperative in the beginning. Finally, however, she began to understand what she needed to do to be a good parent. She had earned participation with the parenting group in a trip to Chicago. For this trip, each parent was given $20 to spend on themselves. Telling me about the gifts, the teacher explained that she was not a mother who showed affection to her children, rarely hugged them. On the last day of class, the mother called through the window for the teacher and her assistant to come down to where she was outside the building. When they got there, she had pins for each of them that she had bought in Chicago with the money given to her. Pleased and surprised, the teacher asked, "Why didn't you spend that money on yourself?" The parent replied, "You two were the only people that have ever cared about me." Then she let the teacher give her a quick hug. This story is an example of how caring by the teacher over the years was received by the mother, as confirmed by the reciprocal mutuality of her gifts and words. When parents and students feel cared for, growth and miracles happen.

SUMMARY AND CONCLUSIONS

At both Harrison School and Newfield School, a happy convergence exists among what teachers think children need to be academically successful, the support teachers believe children need from the principal, and the support the children and teachers get from the principals. Both schools offer to their students what the staff members believe the children need: a combination of emotional support, high expectations, enrichment of their experiences, programs for their parents, compassion for them as individuals, and instructional programs and strategies that offer consistent procedures as well as hands-on exciting teaching. As principals, Aurthur Perkins and Carmen Perez-Dickson do what staff members believe educational leaders should do for children living in poverty: obtain funding and other resources to enhance teaching and learning; act as mentors and role models; offer love, constructive criticism, and emotional support; provide opportunities for experience to build the knowledge they lack; and connect strongly with parents both through programs and relationships. Staff members feel supported by both women in the following ways: appreciation, communication, and backing them up; ability to take charge; above-and-beyond effort; clear vision and high expectations; skills with parents; and being an exemplar.

Aurthur Perkins and Carmen Perez-Dickson emerge from faculty and staff descriptions as leaders who provide caring support, strength and toughness, the grounding of spiritual values, personal dynamism, and thoughtful intelligence. They understand that without the genuine caring for all involved in the school community, any programmatic or curricular efforts to enhance learning will meet with limited success. The work of teaching children who have so much potential and, in many instances, so far to go is emotionally and intellectually demanding. Both principals as well as Harrison and Newfield faculty and staff members clearly understand that the learning successes of their schools emerge from the widespread belief in and pervasive caring at each school for the children and their families.

Chapter Five

Leadership of High-Performing, High-Poverty Schools: The Research Context

Researchers individually and in teams have studied high-poverty schools where learning of students exceeds expectations. Some recent national, widely publicized, and well-funded studies suggest that the reasons for student success have to do with technical strategies and factors such as measurable goals, curriculum aligned with learning standards, increasing instructional time in reading and math, and accountability systems (Barth, Haycock, Jackson, Mora, Ruiz, Robinson, and Wilkins 1999; Carlson, Shagle-Shah, and Ramirez 1999; Carter 2002a, 2002b; Johnson and Asera 1999). On the other hand, case studies have focused on leaders who abandon deficit thinking about the children and who practice strong relational leadership that affects attitudes and empowers teachers (Quint 1994; Reyes, Scribner, and Scribner 1999; Riester, Pursch, and Skrla 2002; Scheurich 1998). In this chapter, the research is organized in terms of four topics: the achievement gap, successful high-poverty schools, strategies of principals in successful high-poverty schools, and beliefs of principals in successful high-poverty schools.

THE ACHIEVEMENT GAP

The achievement gap is difficult to describe. On the basis of a vast array of test score data, Miller (1995) contends that the gap has been not just a phenomenon of the last three decades but a twentieth-century trend. Documentation of the achievement gap in the 1960s was one of the factors that led to school integration. Initially, the gap was described in terms of white and African American students, with Latinos now included in the term *minority achievement gap*. Miller explains, "By the mid-1980s, a number of reform reports had begun to address the persistent gaps in academic achievement between majority students and those from several minority groups—especially African Americans, Latinos, and Native Americans" (1995, 1). In considering the resurgence of segregation in American schools, Orfield, Frankenberg, and Lee write, "After more than 60 years of trying to implement the 1896 mandate of 'separate but equal,' followed by a third of a century of Title I programs trying to improve high-poverty schools, both race and poverty remain powerfully linked to educational inequality. Schools faced with both high minority enrollments and high poverty rates rarely excel" (2002–2003, 19). Recent scholars speak about the achievement gap in terms of both low-income and minority students. Progress in reducing the gap was made between 1970 and 1988, but it has been widening steadily ever since. "The reversal is evident in grades, test scores, dropout rates, and other indicators, and it has taken place in every type of school district and in all socioeconomic groups" (Nieto 2002–2003, 8). According to a recent Gallup poll, 95 percent of the public says that closing the gap is important, and 29 percent (up from 21 percent a year ago) "say the achievement gap is mostly caused by the quality of schooling that students receive" (Scherer 2002–2003, 5).

Some describe the gap in terms of test scores, others in terms of years of schooling completed; still others speak of long-term consequences for employment. For example, Haycock (2002–2003) writes:

> At the fourth grade level approximately two-thirds of African American and Latino youngsters perform below the basic level on the National Assessment of Education Progress in reading, compared with only 28 percent of white students. In mathematics, more than 53 percent of Latino students and 62 percent of African American students perform below basic; for white students, the number below basic is about 22 percent. By 8th grade, most African American and Latino students have mastered those very basic skills, but white students have gone on to master higher-level skills. By the conclusion of high school, African American and Latino students have skills— in both reading and mathematics—that are virtually identical to those of white students at the end of middle school. (13–14)

From a different perspective, Scherer (2002–2003) explains that both African Americans and Latinos are less likely to graduate from high school, earn a college degree, or earn enough to be middle-class than are whites. Referring to different income prospects for African Americans than for whites, Scherer reports that they are three times more likely to be poor and twice as likely to be unemployed.

Reasons for the Achievement Gap

The causes of the achievement gap remain unknown with any level of certainty, but commonly identified contributing factors can be listed. For example, Singham cites "biased standardized tests that do not match the learning style of black students, less money spent on educating black students, socioeconomic differences, lack of motivation, negative peer pressure, lack of family support for education, teacher biases" (2003, 587). As explanations for the achievement gap, he considers each of these commonly listed factors to be myths that, like all myths, contain elements of truth. In an article addressing the Latino achievement gap, Valverde and Scribner (2001) advance a different list: less-qualified teachers, fewer expendable resources per student, lowered expectations for student achievement, more and harsher discipline (a possible reflection of racial stereotyping), mismatches between home and school culture, and high mobility rates of students and teachers. As an afterthought, they add that the schools "tend to be located in communities with high poverty rates and more low-income families" (23). Interestingly, only two items on the lists are the same—less money spent and teacher biases.

Because urban minority students tend to be from low-income families, some educators have viewed poverty to be the cause of the achievement gap. Miller (1995) states that the difficulty in understanding whether the gap is a racial/ethnic issue or a poverty issue is because many earlier studies only looked at the racial/ethnic factor. Biddle (2001) concurs. In reality, the gap can be analyzed from a variety of perspectives, including educational, economic, sociological, psychological, and cross-cultural, to name only a few alternatives. More recently, some studies have looked at the interaction of race/ethnicity and socioeconomic status with achievement. According to Singham, "Traditional measures of socioeconomic status (consisting of income, wealth, and parental education) account for at most one-third of the gap" (2003, 587). This assessment cannot be regarded as the whole truth, however, about the size of poverty's effect on the achievement gap. Biddle (2001) discusses the factors confounding research about the degree to which

poverty affects school achievement—including, for example, research design flaws, incomplete information from schools, and confused measures of
poverty. He concludes:

> A number of good studies have recently appeared in which the net educa-
> tional effects of poverty are addressed directly. These studies have found
> that poverty, indeed, has substantial and negative effects on education, al-
> though the size of those effects varies depending on the type of educational
> outcome examined, the grade level studied, whether the poverty experi-
> enced is transitory or long term, and whether we are studying effects among
> individuals or larger human assemblies. In short, logic and evidence both
> suggest that when America tolerates a massive, uniquely high level of child-
> hood poverty, it also imposes unfair educational disadvantages on many of
> its citizens. (8–9)

Remedies for the Achievement Gap

In contrast to the uncertainty about causes for the achievement gap, remedies are advocated with great certainty. What is seen as the remedy typically stems from an interpretation of what causes the gap, but single-
focus remedies have not been sufficient. From a different point of view,
Singham suggests that we focus not on the gap, but elsewhere; that if we
must focus on a gap, then "the gap we should be focusing on is the difference between where *all* [italics added] students are now and where we
believe they should be" (2003, 589). His rationale is based on a study of
strong implementation of a reform in a high school math curriculum that
"narrowed the gaps between whites and underrepresented minorities,
while improving the performance of both groups on all categories" (588).
His perspective generally is that quality teaching is the best approach to
closing the achievement gap.

Haycock would agree: "It turns out that what schools do make a huge
difference in whether students learn. And what matters most is good
teachers" (2002–2003, 13). Other recommendations associated with quality teachers describe the importance of teachers who practice culturally
relevant, culturally responsive, culturally proficient, or culturally sensitive
pedagogy (Delpit 1995; Gay 2000; Ladson-Billings 1994; Nieto
2002–2003; Valverde and Scribner 2001). Bonding of the community and

school, with teachers taking on parental roles with the students, has been identified as an approach to closing the achievement gap (Morris 2002). That teachers need to believe their minority and low-income students capable of academic achievement at a high level is one factor about which there is little disagreement. For example, Valverde and Scribner write, "Unless their teachers firmly believe that students of color can learn, they will not" (2001, 24). Some state this concept of believing in the capability of the students in terms of the abandonment of deficit thinking (Shields 2003; Wagstaff and Fusarelli 1995). Similarly, writing about three within-school models used by high schools successful in closing the achievement gap, Jackson (2003) states:

> All three models create self-contained environments of unusual student engagement and high academic achievement. They are staffed by committed teachers with an infectious enthusiasm for their subject matter who communicate a caring concern for their students as individuals, combined with a conviction that they can accomplish more than the students themselves believe possible. (583)

Addressing the issue of teacher expectations and the teacher quality gap, Singham writes, "Compounding this gap in teaching quality is the fact that the impact of teacher expectations is three times as great for blacks as for whites and also larger for girls and for children from low-income families. Interestingly, the ethnicity of the teacher has little effect on student performance" (2003, 589). Also associated with improving teaching are recommendations for more collaboration and grade-level teaming (Carter and Fenwick 2001; Frank 2003) and sustained professional development programs (Singham 2003).

Miller (1995) lists twenty-six proposals to improve the education of minorities and thus reduce the achievement gap. On his list are actions that are directly concerned with improving the educational system, as well as those that address the broader economic and social problems associated with low achievement. Examples of ideas for schools include more early childhood programs, multicultural curricula, improved teacher education programs, more minority teachers, elimination of all tracking of students, improving bilingual education, and developing new academic evaluation tools and systems.

SUCCESSFUL HIGH-POVERTY SCHOOLS

According to Miller's (1995) historical review of the experiences of minority students in American schools, the Coleman report stimulated the search for effective schools. Published in 1966, the controversial Coleman report was thought to provide evidence that integration of African American children into the public schools would have little or no effect on their academic achievement, that schools could not make a difference in the education of poor and minority children, even though Coleman and his colleagues did not say this. "One of the principal findings of the Coleman report was that variations in standardized test scores among students from different racial/ethnic groups were strongly associated with variations in social-class-related characteristics, for example, parent education level" (Miller 1995, 143–44). An interpretation of the report was that the homes students come from made a greater difference to their educational achievement than the schools they attended.

Educators responded to the Coleman report by looking for effective schools, "schools that did close a meaningful part of the academic achievement gap between poor and middle-class students as well as between whites and minorities, by strategies that other schools could learn to use" (Miller 1995, 237). One such response was that of Edmonds (1979), who first identified two schools that did not fit with Coleman's results because students in these two low-income schools were performing better than peers in more affluent schools nearby. The effective schools research continued and developed in stages, focusing first on schools exceptional for their student performance, considering the school demographics (Edmonds 1986). Many descriptive studies of individual effective schools were completed. In the 1980s, networks of researchers and practitioners identified common traits and processes in the schools. These became known as the effective schools correlates, because they were seen to correlate with high levels of student achievement and appeared consistently in high-performing schools regardless of the backgrounds of the students. Correlates of success identified in these studies were a safe and orderly environment, a climate of high expectations for success, strong instructional leadership by the principal, frequent monitoring of student progress, a clear and focused mission, opportunities to learn and time on task, and good home-school relations. Other initiatives focused on improving educational opportunities for poor and minority children developed in the period of school reform beginning in the 1980s were the Coalition of Essential Schools developed by Theodore Sizer of Brown University, the Accelerated Schools Project developed by Henry M. Levin of Stanford University, the School Development Program developed by James Comer of Yale University, and the Central Park East elementary schools developed by Deborah Meier (Miller 1995).

A recent national study of successful high-poverty schools coincided with the impending reauthorization of Title I. The purpose of the report, *Dispelling the Myth* (Barth et al. 1999), was to look at successful high-poverty schools. This report from Education Trust in collaboration with the Council of Chief State School Officers dispelled the myth that high-poverty schools fail, demonstrating instead many successes. A total of twenty-one states volunteered to be included in the study. Surveys were mailed to 1,200 elementary and secondary schools identified as high-performing, high-poverty schools. The information in the report was compiled from 366 schools that responded to the survey and included rural and urban schools. The percentage of low-income students in the schools ranged from over 50 percent to over 75 percent. The report seemed to validate the policies that had been promoted by the 1994 Title I law and researchers determined that the following elements led to the successes of these high-poverty schools:

1. Use of state standards extensively to design curriculum and instruction, assess student work, and evaluate teachers
2. Increase instructional time in reading and math in order to help students meet standards
3. Devote a larger proportion of funds to support professional development focused on changing instructional practice
4. Implement comprehensive systems to monitor individual student progress and provide extra support to students as soon as needed
5. Focus their efforts to involve parents in helping students meet standards
6. Have state or district accountability systems in place that have real consequences for adults in the schools (Barth et al. 1999, 2–3)

Not every school had all six of these characteristics, but most had some. The most significant finding was considered to be the extent to which the schools were using standards to design curricula and assess student work. A majority (78 percent) had extended learning time in core subjects, such as reading and math. A third of these schools were allocating 10 percent of Title I monies to professional development. A majority of respondents (81 percent) reported a comprehensive system to monitor student progress and provide early intervention to students deemed to be falling behind. Accountability systems for adults in schools were less common, reported in fewer than 50 percent of the schools. Parent involvement increasingly was being focused on activities associated with student achievement. With regard to the 1994 reauthorization of Title I, 79 percent of respondents had adopted schoolwide programs, and 56 percent had control of all their Title I dollars. According to the report, these schools on average had enrollments "in excess of 60 percent white, 17 percent African American, 13 percent Latino, 2 percent Asian, and 4 percent Native American" (12). The only direct comment about leadership was that each school was led by a principal who had served an average of 4.5 years at the school. Other studies of successful high-poverty schools have focused on the strategies and beliefs of the principals.

STRATEGIES OF PRINCIPALS IN SUCCESSFUL HIGH-POVERTY SCHOOLS

Recent major studies focused more directly on the leadership of principals have included *Leave No Child Behind*, a report prepared by the Chicago Schools Academic Accountability Council (Carlson, Shagle-Shah, and Ramirez 1999); a national report called *Hope for Urban Education* based on successes of nine urban elementary schools (Johnson and Asera 1999); and two publications from research sponsored by the Heritage Foundation titled *No Excuses*—one report focused on the study of twenty-one high-performing, high-poverty schools (Carter 2002b) and another focused on seven principals from these schools (Carter 2002a).

Leave No Child Behind

In Chicago, the second wave of school reform that began in 1995 focused on improving reading. The Chicago Schools Academic Accountability

Council focused a two-year study on leadership strategies of principals in thirty-two elementary schools where students' Iowa Test of Basic Skills (ITBS) reading scores had increased the most. The thirteen common strategies identified by the principals of these most-improved schools were reported in *Leave No Child Behind* (Carlson, Shagle-Shah, and Ramirez 1999). As stated in the report:

> The data demonstrate that students can flourish academically regardless of their background and that race, poverty and other urban challenges are not reasons for academic failure. They demonstrate that schools with a large percent of students coming from low income and minority backgrounds can be very successful if the local conditions and school leadership are right. (11)

The principals of these thirty-two improving schools identified a pattern of common strategies for being successful in improving reading. The report details how the principals implemented the following strategies (Carlson, Shagle-Shah, and Ramirez 1999, 13–26):

1. Create a consistent reading program
2. Set clear goals and standards
3. Coordinate curriculum
4. Build strong team faculty
5. Hold teachers accountable
6. Monitor both students and teachers
7. Foster individual teacher support
8. Encourage professional development
9. Ensure philosophical consistency
10. Invest in performance
11. Instill a love of learning through reading
12. Work together
13. Increase time on task

Focusing specifically on characteristics of leadership, Carlson, Shagle-Shah, and Ramirez (1999) describe the principals as passionate, hands-on, responsive leaders who are visionary, set goals, and are good at both politics and management. They are in communication with their teachers and in classrooms often. They know what is going on in their buildings. Of the thirty-two principals, seventeen were women and fifteen were men.

Hope for Urban Education

The Hope for Urban Education project (Johnson and Asera 1999) investigated the success of nine urban elementary schools serving mostly children of color, located in Boston, San Antonio, Atlanta, East St. Louis, Detroit, Milwaukee, Houston, Chicago, and Cheverly (metropolitan Washington, D.C.), Maryland. Schools selected for the report had a majority of low-income students, with seven of the schools having at least 80 percent low-income students. Three years of assessment data were used to select these high-performing schools where student achievement in mathematics and reading was higher than the average of all schools in the state, or higher than the 50th percentile on nationally normed tests. Case studies were written for each of the schools to tell the story of how each school changed to become high performing. In each school, four types of change were identified: changing the school climate, changing academic instruction, changing relationships with parents and the community, and changing the organization of schooling. Generally, the report identified important change strategies used by multiple schools. These strategies are:

1. Targeting an important, visible, attainable first goal
2. Refocusing energies on service to children
3. Building students' sense of responsibility for appropriate behavior and creating an environment in which students are likely to behave well
4. Creating a collective sense of responsibility for improvement
5. Increasing instructional leadership
6. Aligning instruction to standards and assessments
7. Getting teachers the resources and training perceived necessary to teach
8. Creating opportunities for teachers to work, plan, and learn together
9. Winning the confidence and respect of parents and building partnerships with them
10. Creating additional time for instruction
11. Persisting through difficulties, setbacks, and failures (Johnson and Asera 1999, 10–22)

All nine of the schools had Title I schoolwide programs. They were schools that did not exempt large numbers of children from state assessments because of language abilities or disabilities of other kinds. There were important differences among the schools: size, grade spans, ethnic composition, rate of improvement, and whether they had used comprehensive school reform models. Even though only two used national models, components of comprehensive school reform were demonstrated. "For instance, many of the schools sought to use research-based practices, provide intensive professional development, ensure the buy-in and support of teachers and other school staff, and secure the backing of the district administration" (1999, 8). Other variations existed in terms of their relationship with their district offices and teacher turnover during the reform process. Seven of the nine schools had women principals.

No Excuses

The Heritage Foundation produced two reports as a result of its sponsored research on high-performing, high-poverty schools. One report (Carter 2002b) synthesized the lessons uncovered from the common practices of twenty-one principals in high-performing, high-poverty schools. The other report (Carter 2002a) featured seven of those principals who take *no excuses* for not meeting the standards of excellence. The study included elementary, middle, and high schools. All schools in the study average above the 65th percentile on national, norm-referenced tests even though in each school 75 percent or more of the students qualify for free or reduced-price lunch. The schools were selected from recommendations from the Department of Education Blue Ribbon Schools Program. Consultation narrowed the list of prospective schools to 400. From this list, 125 schools with the highest concentrations of low-income students and academic excellence were identified. The twenty-one schools in the study came from that list. Most but not all are public schools.

Research findings indicated seven common elements and leadership traits that led to the success of these schools:

1. Principals must be free [to spend their school budgets as they see fit].
2. Principals use measurable goals to establish a culture of achievement.
3. Master teachers bring out the best in a faculty.
4. Rigorous and regular testing leads to continuous student achievement.
5. Achievement is the key to discipline.

6. Principals work actively with parents to make the home a center of learning.
7. Effort creates ability. (Carter 2002a, 5–8)

These seven elements are the foundation for what the report identifies as *best practices*. These best practices involve changes "in the way our schools involve their parents, train their teachers, test their students, teach their children, and spend their money" (Carter 2002b, 13). The tone differs from the other reports, perhaps a reflection of the political agenda of the Heritage Foundation. The schools have been successful in transforming the attitudes of parents, of educating parents to be committed to academic excellence. In many of the schools, parents sign contracts or covenants pledging specific kinds of support for their children. Some of the schools provide literacy programs for parents and hold parenting workshops. Each school assumes responsibility for getting teachers the professional development to be successful. Although the schools may not automatically get assigned the best teachers, they work to turn the teachers they have into the best. Schools emphasize teamwork and the sharing of best practices among teachers. Almost without exception, the principals of these schools believe that poor test scores reflect poor teaching. Said one principal, "You either believe your children can learn—and you give the test to prove it—or you don't" (2002b, 24). These are schools where teachers focus on basic skills first because of the belief that the children will not be successful without first mastering basic skills of reading, mathematics, writing, and speaking. Principals of these schools manage their money so that expenditures will support student performance. Typically, they spend money on curricula, adding instructional support and materials, and on teachers who are rewarded for excellence either through bonuses, performance for pay, or staff development opportunities.

Comparative Analysis

As could be expected, given the emphasis on teacher quality as a remedy for the achievement gap, the teachers emerged as the one category for which all four recent national reports contained recommendations. In *Dispelling the Myth* (Barth et al. 1999), *Leave No Child Behind* (Carlson, Shagle-Shah, and Ramirez 1999), *Hope for Urban Education* (Johnson and Asera 1999), and

No Excuses (Carter 2002a, 2002b), teachers were recognized as central to the learning and achievement of students in high-poverty schools. Recommendations of the reports included getting teachers the resources they needed, providing training and professional development, creating opportunities for teachers to work together, and doing everything possible to provide the highest quality teachers. These are all actions that can be seen in the leadership practices of Perkins and Perez-Dickson. Four other categories of recommendations were addressed in three of the reports: goals, working with parents, testing and monitoring, and curriculum design.

In the category of goals, best practices included clarity, instilling a love of learning, working together, and philosophical consistency (Carlson, Shagle-Shah, and Ramirez 1999); creating a collective sense of responsibility for improvement, targeting an important visible and attainable first goal, and refocusing energies on service to children (Johnson and Asera 1999); principals using measurable goals to establish a culture of achievement, and the recognition that effort creates ability (Carter 2002a). Again, these actions are visible in the leadership practices of Perkins and Perez-Dickson. From three reports, the best-practices recommendations for working with parents focused on involving parents as partners in helping the students learn (Barth et al. 1999; Carter 2002a, 2002b; Johnson and Asera 1999), with which Perkins and Perez-Dickson agree. The best-practices recommendations for testing and monitoring from three reports were also similar, advocating the importance of the assessment to learning (Barth et al. 1999; Carlson, Shagle-Shah, and Ramirez 1999; Carter 2002a, 2002b). Only one report emphasized the importance of using monitoring to identify students in need of extra support so that help could be provided as soon as possible (Barth et al. 1999). This is a practice followed by Perkins in the regular meetings with faculty by grade level. Finally, in three of the reports, the importance of a curriculum coordinated and aligned with state standards and assessments was stated (Barth et al. 1999; Carlson, Shagle-Shah, and Ramirez 1999; Johnson and Asera 1999). Perkins meets individually and in groups with teachers to work on alignment of state standards with the Harrison curriculum. Speaking of that nine-year process at the school, one teacher said:

> No one in this area has adjusted to the changes in their own job, to the changing face of how the state looks at education, as well as Mrs. Perkins has. We were always ahead, and that started with her. We understood that

the standardized test would be basically the only way that our performance as teachers would be measured. Most of us believe that we are a lot more than what some standardized test says. . . . Because of Mrs. Perkins and the staff, we got ourselves together so that we were always a step ahead of these trends, and so we got a spike in our test scores as a result of that hard work.

Two of the reports addressed the importance of a principal investing dollars wisely in resources and training that would support student achievement (Carlson, Shagle-Shah, and Ramirez 1999; Carter 2002a, 2002b). Both Perkins and Perez-Dickson have brought large grants to their schools and use the funds to provide focused professional development as well as purchase resources the teachers want. One report addressed the issue of creating an environment that would support learning through a focus on cultivating in students a sense of responsibility for their own behaviors (Johnson and Asera 1999). This is certainly a key in Perkins's approach to discipline. Another report held that achievement was the key to student discipline (Carter 2002a). Three other recommendations were each included in only one of the four reports: increasing instructional leadership (Johnson and Asera 1999); have state or district accountability systems in place that have real consequences for adults in the schools (Barth et al. 1999); emphasize basic skills, and understanding how progressive education has hurt low-income children most of all (Carter 2002b).

BELIEFS OF PRINCIPALS IN
SUCCESSFUL HIGH-POVERTY SCHOOLS

Reports from four qualitative individual and multisite case studies arrive at similar conclusions to the previously discussed studies in terms of the centrality of teachers to student success and the importance of working in partnership with parents. Of the studies previously discussed, however, only two mention the importance of believing in the abilities of the students. The *No Excuses* (Carter 2002a) principals operate from that belief in insisting on high-level, rigorous curricula. Editors of the *Hope for Urban Education* report (Johnson and Asera 1999) approach the issue of attitudes, albeit indirectly, in stating the importance of "refocusing energies on service to children." On the other hand, each of the following case studies (Quint 1994; Reyes, Scribner, and Scribner 1999; Riester, Pursch, and Skrla 2002; Scheurich 1998) emphasizes personal relational leadership and the role of the principal in bringing about abandonment of an attitude of deficit thinking about the children and their abilities. "All the strategies in the world will not help to close the achievement gap if you don't believe it can be done" (Bell 2002–2003, 32).

Schooling Homeless Children

Quint's (1994) *Schooling Homeless Children* is based on her qualitative case study dissertation. The book tells the story of what happened after Carole Williams, African American principal of B. F. Day Elementary in Seattle, decided to confront her own ignorance about the lives of low-income children attending her school. Making house calls in the community, she discovered that a significant number of the children and their families were, in fact, homeless. She experienced a dramatic personal awakening in her own understanding of the defiant and disruptive behaviors of many of the students. An at-school suicide attempt of a young boy and further reflection about a decision she made to restrict the other children from using the drinking fountain on the main floor of the school, which housed the Orca program for gifted and talented students, caused her to rethink her leadership of the building. The book presents the story of how her leadership, empowered with a new ethical social reconstructionist vision, changed the school's character and took it from the lowest ranking of Seattle's sixty-five elementary schools in academic improvement in 1988–1989 to "7th in improvement in reading, 16th in language arts, and 18th in math" by 1990–1991 (Quint 1994, 6).

Quint (1994) advocates for the reformed B. F. Day Elementary to be a working model for America's public schools. Carole Williams transformed her leadership and school. From her own experiences with going into the streets and neighborhoods, she understood that the staff needed to know the children as individuals and to know their situations in order to teach them well. She provided powerful staff development experiences that caused teachers to reexamine their stereotypes and deficit thinking about the children. Announcing that she had no idea how to better reach the children, she facilitated the working together of the staff to discover the way. She found the time for teachers to work together and ways for them to learn what they did not know about the children and how to teach them. Quint observes about the work of Carole Williams, "As the staff came to understand that learning takes place in relationships, and that children very much want to please the 'significant adults' in their lives, the students began to show marked improvement in academic achievement and socialization. The climate for learning was set" (103). The climate for learning was supported by restructuring that included development of powerful collaborations with community partners, and even the addition of community-based staff members in the school.

With teachers at its heart, Williams created what Quint (1994) calls a *coalescence of significant adults* that succeeded in bringing about large-scale change. The school became and began to call itself a *family school,* breaking the previous bureaucratic mold of doing things to become welcoming, inclusive, and responsive to the learning needs of family members as well as the children. Most importantly, this coalescence of significant adults made it their business to find for families the basic resources many had not been able to develop for themselves. Working through community partners and using case management strategies, they found homes, food, job training, and employment opportunities in their efforts to support the children and their families. The school staff extended caring and respect to the family members as well as the students.

Highly Successful and Loving, Public Elementary Schools Populated Mainly by Low-SES Children of Color

Scheurich presents what he calls a superior model for the education of low-SES children of color that was "developed at the grassroots level of education by school-level educators, principally educators of color who were working essentially on their own" (1998, 452). Whereas all the principals were persons of color, the staffs of their schools represented all races. Scheurich calls the model HiPass (High Performance All Student Success) because the children in these genuinely caring and child-centered schools succeed at a level that is equal to many of the high-performing Anglo schools in Texas. He does not present the model as a formula that can be applied in every school but as an example of what can happen when schools are responsive to the children they serve. The research that documented the model involved teams of researchers and four sources or sets of data gathered and analyzed over a period of years in Texas schools.

Principals in these schools clearly did not participate in deficit thinking about the children and their families. In Scheurich's words, "These grass-roots educators, particularly the principals, were simply unwilling to accept the widespread negative assumptions about the children in their schools, and they were unwilling to accept any other course of action than one that would lead to the highest levels of academic success" (433–34). The foundation for the academic success of the students in these schools lies in five core beliefs that are interrelated:

1. All children can succeed at high academic levels—no exceptions allowed.
2. Child- or learner-centered schools.
3. All children must be treated with love, appreciation, care, and respect—no exceptions allowed.
4. The racial culture, including the first language of the child, is always highly valued—no exceptions allowed.
5. The school exists for and serves the community—there is little separation. (Scheurich 1998, 460–65)

In addition to the core beliefs, Scheurich (1998) identified seven interwoven cultural characteristics that the schools have in common:

1. A strong shared vision.
2. Loving, caring environments for children and adults.
3. Strongly collaborative—"We are a family."
4. Innovative, experimental, openness to new ideas.
5. Hardworking but not burning out.
6. Appropriate conduct is built into the organizational culture.
7. School staff as a whole hold themselves accountable for the success of all children. (467–75)

These cultural characteristics and the belief that all children can succeed at high academic levels could also be used to describe the transformed culture of B. F. Day Elementary in Seattle (Quint 1994). Scheurich understands the model to be situated in the cultural norms of communities of color and "their lived, historical struggles to first survive and then to create powerful, loving, communal spaces for themselves and their children" (457). He writes about the principals, "It was their deep love for their children and their passionate commitment to making a difference for those children that created the model" (454).

Lessons from High-Performing Hispanic Schools

Reyes, Scribner, and Scribner (1999) edited a book reporting on an extensive study focused on eight highly successful schools serving low-income Hispanic students living along the Texas–Mexico border region between Brownsville and Laredo. Three elementary, three middle, and two high schools were chosen for the qualitative case studies that were conducted by teams of researchers. A common theme among these schools is that all community members were committed to doing their best "through individual growth and mutual learning" (Scribner 1999, 12). Scribner proposes that four dimensions support the development of learning communities in schools for linguistically and culturally diverse students. These major dimensions are:

1. Collaborative governance and leadership
2. Community and family involvement
3. Culturally responsive pedagogy
4. Advocacy-oriented assessment (Scribner 1999, 12–15)

Collaborative governance and leadership created climates of caring and innovation, where decisions were based on giving the students the instruction that would work to ensure their learning successes. Communication and collaboration involved administrators, professional staff, and the community. Principals operated as facilitators, were highly visible, built trust, and went the extra mile as they upheld a clear and coherent mission and vision of success for the students. Professional development opportunities and staying current with the research literature were keys to the teachers' successes in the classroom. The schools featured an ethic of caring along with belief in the potential of the students and "explicit denial of the cultural deprivation argument" (Wagstaff and Fusarelli 1999, 34).

Collaborative relationships with parents were a critical element in the successes of the schools. Parents were respected, welcomed, and valued in formal and informal ways. In return, the parents valued the schools and were able to show through their involvement their concern for the development of their children. Parents volunteered in schools to provide good role models for the students, and they valued their association with the school and the other parents. Five categories of best practices were identified in these high-performing Hispanic schools (Scribner, Young, and Pedroza 1999, 52):

1. Build on cultural values of Hispanic parents
2. Stress personal contact with parents
3. Foster communication with parents
4. Create a warm environment for parents
5. Facilitate structural accommodations for parent involvement

Structural accommodations included having parent centers on the campuses, teaming with parents, and organizing parent advisory committees.

Culturally responsive pedagogy and advocacy-oriented assessment work together to support student success. The book presents information about culturally responsive pedagogies in math and reading. Teachers do believe that every student has the ability to achieve and they communicate that belief with students and parents. Instruction includes goal-directed activities and instructional conversations that encourage higher-order thinking skill development. Students are assumed to bring to the classroom important "funds of knowledge" that teachers then use to form the basis of their instructional strategies (Scribner and Reyes 1999, 203). Assessment at the classroom level is valued. When students fail to perform on standardized assessments, instead of assuming that the students are at fault, advocacy-oriented assessment practices instead question the test and the classroom or testing conditions first, and then work to alter those productively. Instructional interventions and modifications are common, resources are maximized through collaboration, and ongoing professional growth of teachers is a given. The authors conclude that an adaptation of the learning community framework developed by Senge (1990) provides a conceptual framework for the practices of high-performing Hispanic schools; in the schools they studied, the five disciplines of the learning organization are practiced in varying degrees.

Principals for Social Justice: Leaders of School Success for Children from Low-Income Homes

Writing about schools that are successful learning environments for children from low-income homes, Riester, Pursch, and Skrla assert that "a key feature of principal leadership in these successful schools is the principal's own belief system" (2002, 283). They also state what has been a premise of this book: that there has been "a lack of focused, in-depth research on what their principals do to create such success" (284). Within the context of creating socially just schools, their study looked at the role of principals in influencing just two factors: the development of early literacy programs for every child, and avoidance of inappropriate special education placements. They selected six public elementary schools in the area surrounding the city of San Antonio, where at least 70 percent of the students were from low-income homes. Each school had nonetheless achieved Recognized or Exemplary status during the 1998–1999 school year. The study involved three to four visits to each school over a period of a year. Data came primarily from interviews with the principals, four of whom were women (two Caucasian and two Hispanic) and two were men (African American and Caucasian).

They did not find "specific curricular arrangements, unique teaching strategies, or dramatically different practices" (292). They did find a belief in and commitment to the success of all the children. These beliefs and commitments in each case had contributed to the development of a shared culture in which responsibility for the success of the children was seen as belonging to the school. They described three common themes in how the principals had eradicated deficit thinking at their schools and created a culture of success for all children. These themes are:

1. promoting a democratic school culture;
2. adopting a prescriptive approach to literacy and academic success; and
3. demonstrating a stubborn persistence in "getting there." (Riester, Pursch, and Skrla 2002, 292)

Specifically, these principals used strategies that had striking similarities. They worked through their teachers by empowering them to be innovative, providing professional development, and giving them time to work together. Each worked to establish a vision of success for all children through a balanced combination of pressure and support (Sebring and

Bryk 2000). They gathered data to make decisions about instruction and freed the teachers to make informed decisions about curriculum and instruction using that data. The article does not address how the principals and schools worked with the families of the students. Attention to a democratic school culture, however, implies an acceptance of involvement of the parents as partners in the education of the students.

Comparative Analysis

In all of these case studies of high-performing, high-poverty schools, the authors explicitly stated that leaders either abandoned or did not hold the deficit-thinking model (Valencia 1997) that locates the failures of students in either their own or their families' cognitive or motivational deficiencies. According to the deficit-thinking model, the children who are not succeeding in school are seen as either not trying or not capable. In these schools, as well as Harrison and Newfield, students and their families were given care and respect as teachers hold themselves accountable for the students' learning. This represents a fundamental attitude difference from schools where educators blame the students and their families for low levels of success. In each case, the principals strongly modeled belief in the abilities of the students to succeed academically, as do Perkins and Perez-Dickson. Professional development reinforced this belief and provided teachers information about how to use culturally responsive instructional practices. In three of the case studies, involvement of family in the schools was a primary cultural characteristic, with family members treated with care and respect, as were the children. Involvement of family was implied in the fourth study. Best practices, therefore, centered on modeling belief in the abilities of the students, providing professional development to support the work of the teachers, and creating a family-centered school. The findings in these case studies closely align with our findings from the case studies of Perkins and Perez-Dickson.

CONCLUSIONS

The principals in our case studies, Aurthur Perkins and Carmen Perez-Dickson, have created successful high-poverty schools. In each case, their leadership practices as we have portrayed them in previous chapters extend and clarify research presented in this chapter. Their beliefs and values are central to their successes. The vision or goal in each school is clear, a holistic vision of developing the learning potential of each child academically, personally, and socially. Each woman believes that the children in her school are capable of learning at the highest levels. Staff members who do not share that belief are encouraged to leave. As principals they also use similar strategies. Each supports the teachers in every possible way, from giving empathy to obtaining grant monies for resources to providing meaningful professional development experiences and materials. Each takes curricular alignment with standards, classroom assessments, and state assessments seriously and expects the best from students. Each is particularly skilled at building relationships and rapport with parents. Each school utilizes parent volunteers and welcomes parents into the school as equal partners.

Principals and teachers who believe that the children from families living in poverty can learn and achieve at a high level are central to the success of the children. What is still missing from the research picture, however, is a look at how principals are able to influence beliefs and attitudes of staff members about the ability and potential of the children. Given the confluence of poverty and racial/ethnic minority status, the media, and other socializing influences in our society, most teachers bring to the classroom harmful stereotypes about the poor. Principals are not exempt. Those wanting success for all students, whatever their economic status, often must face their own tendencies to see the potential of low-income students as limited. Carole Williams's story is a good example of a principal taking another look, taking a step back, and starting over from a different perspective (Quint 1994). Having educated themselves, principals then often must educate teachers by engaging them in understanding their own, sometimes preconscious, prejudices and stereotypes about the poor. Only when teachers value the children and their families and believe in the ability of the children to learn will teachers be ready for the hard work of teaching children for whom traditional methods and curricula may not be the best choice.

Chapter Six

Influencing Beliefs and Attitudes

If believing all children can learn is critical to achievement, then beliefs or attitudes to the contrary hold back the academic achievement of children living in poverty. According to Valencia (1997), deficit thinking about poor and minority children, their families, their neighborhoods, and their racial/ethnic cultures has existed in this country for over a century to explain ongoing school failure or disproportionately low academic achievement. From the perspective of deficit thinking, the fault lies not in the teachers, schools, educational system, or structural inequalities of the economy; rather the deficiencies of the children hinder their ability to learn. Deficit thinking is a theory to explain the failures of economically disadvantaged minority students to succeed in school. According to Valencia, "deficit thinking is tantamount to the process of 'blaming the victim.' It is a model founded on imputation, not documentation" (1997, x).

Definitions of the words *belief* and *attitude* reveal important connotations. Belief can be defined as "1. a principle, etc., accepted as true or real, especially without proof. 2. opinion, conviction. 3. religious faith. 4. trust or confidence, as in a person's abilities, etc." (McLeod 1987, 86). Attitude can be defined as "1. a mental view or disposition, especially as it indicates opinion or allegiance. . . . 3. a position of the body indicating mood or emotion . . ." (McLeod 1987, 60). According to these definitions, essentially our beliefs and attitudes are matters of opinion that affect both our actions and interactions, and are reflected in nonverbal behaviors. Opinions can change. The purpose of this chapter is twofold: (1) to explore how beliefs and attitudes about poor and minority children may be problematic for many educators who want to help children learn; and (2) to consider how principals might approach influencing faculty and staff members affected by deficit thinking toward more productive beliefs and attitudes about the worth and learning abilities of children from families living in poverty.

We begin the chapter with a look at the larger context, followed by a brief history of the theory of deficit thinking that has influenced stereotypes, social policy, and educational practice. We consider how a leader might approach influencing negative beliefs and attitudes about persons living in poverty. The chapter ends with a discussion of survey results from Harrison and Newfield about attitudes of educators toward poverty, a look at the challenges and rewards they experience teaching in high-poverty schools, and our conclusions.

THE LARGER CONTEXT

What is the evidence that deficit thinking on the part of educators is hampering abilities of students to learn? An answer to that question must include a look at stereotypes about racial and ethnic minority groups as well as typical beliefs and attitudes about poverty. The historical and contemporary reality is that members of minority groups live in poverty in disproportionate numbers.

Contemporary Racial and Ethnic Prejudice

The evidence of continuing racial and ethnic prejudice can be found in the persistence of hereditarianism, blaming the victim, the construct of the underclass, and the prevalence of "at-risk" discourse. Valencia and Solorzano (1997) write:

> What is most disturbing, we feel, is the apparent pervasiveness among the general public of such beliefs held toward minority groups. Results from a 1990 national survey conducted by the National Opinion Research Center at the University of Chicago showed there is strong evidence that a substantial proportion of white Americans still cling to racial stereotypes of a deficit nature. (198)

Prejudice can be defined as "1. an opinion formed beforehand, especially an unfavorable one based on inadequate facts. 2. the act or condition of holding such opinions. 3. intolerance of or dislike for people of a specific race, religion, etc." (McLeod 1987, 778). Prejudices are often based on stereotypes used to describe members of a particular group. "Stereotypes may include positive, negative, and neutral attributes and characteristics, some of which may be largely accurate and some completely inaccurate" (Miller 1995, 178). According to Miller, social science researchers have found that while blacks and whites tend to have positive images of themselves, the traits they list for each other tend to be predominantly negative or neutral.

Reviewing trend data on whites' beliefs regarding the intelligence of blacks, Miller (1995) reports a series of surveys beginning in 1939. In 1939, more than 5,000 Americans surveyed by Roper for *Fortune* magazine were asked, "Do you think Negroes now generally have higher intelligence than white people, lower, or about the same?" According to Miller, "about 71 percent of those interviewed indicated that they thought blacks were less intelligent than whites, 22 percent indicated that they thought that blacks and whites had about the same intelligence, less than 1 percent indicated that blacks were more intelligent than whites, and 6 percent indicated that they did not know" (179). Follow-up questions ascertained that "47 percent of the entire national sample of Americans held the view that blacks were innately less intelligent than whites" (179). Beginning in 1942, periodic national surveys of the attitudes of whites toward blacks were conducted by the National Opinion Research Center (NORC) at the University of Chicago. In 1942, only 42 percent of whites indicated "that they thought blacks were as intelligent as whites" (179). "By 1956, 78 percent of the whites indicated that they thought African Americans and whites were of equal intelligence, and only about 20 percent indicated that they thought that blacks were less intelligent than whites" (180).

This pattern of increasingly favorable estimates of blacks' intelligence continued through the final NORC survey in 1968. Results of polls conducted by Harris from the 1970s to 1991 continued the trend, with the 1991 Harris poll finding that only 11 percent of whites believed that blacks had less native intelligence than whites. Although not a steadily upward trend, with results varying depending upon how the question was worded, "over the past half-century, the view that blacks are innately less intelligent than whites seems to have become much less widely held within the general white adult population" (Miller 1995, 181). Miller expresses the opinion, however, that the "surveys have recorded a somewhat larger shift in whites' views on the innate intellectual ability of blacks than may have actually taken place" (181) because after segregation was no longer legally sanctioned, persons might have chosen not to express opinions about perceived inferiority of African Americans so freely.

The whole challenging big picture emerges when one considers other surveys from the 1990s that contained questions about cultural inferiority. In 1990, Kluegel compiled a synthesis of data from an annual General Society Survey (GSS) also conducted by NORC. Looking at responses to why blacks have worse jobs, income, and housing than whites, his aggregated data revealed "that more than two in five whites believed that lack of motivation was entirely or partially responsible for poverty among blacks" (Miller 1995, 183). Approximately 30 percent of those surveyed "relied exclusively on a combination of genetic and cultural theories of inferiority to explain why blacks were doing less well than whites in 1988–89. . . . About 65 percent of whites relied on the genetic and cultural theories in combination with discrimination and lack of educational opportunity to explain this phenomenon" (183). Miller summarized, "About 57 percent of all *nonblacks* in the 1990 GSS indicated a belief that blacks are less intelligent than whites. This is the same percentage found to hold this view in the Jackman-Senter survey of 1975. On the basis of these two results, we can estimate that 50–60 percent of whites held this view as the 1990s began" (185). Stereotypes are remarkably persistent, as Miller explains:

> Research suggests that once a stereotype is formed, individuals are likely to note and regard information that seems to support the stereotype as confirmation of its validity and to ignore or discard information that is not consistent with the stereotype rather than change the stereotype in a significant way. . . . The current high poverty and welfare rates among African Americans, along with their lower levels of educational attainment and academic achievement, may feed preexisting beliefs in their innate or cultural inferiority. (199)

Miller concludes, therefore, "one should not be surprised by the resiliency of notions of the inferiority of African Americans and other minority groups" (201).

Beliefs about Causes of Poverty

False assumptions are made that people who live in poverty remain poor because of their own inadequacies. However, the truth is that "poverty is perpetuated by stereotypes which misrepresent reality, by the historic dependence of our society on the employed poor built into inherited institutional structures, by the failure of those in power to recognize the true dimensions of poverty's long-term blight, by the many ways in which the poverty sector benefits the non-poor" (Chamberlin 2001, 70). Wilson writes, "Despite the slight increase in the support for structural explanations of the causes of poverty, Americans remain strongly disposed to the idea that individuals are largely responsible for their economic conditions" (1996, 160). Evidence suggests that beliefs of educators toward causes of poverty are similar (Drazen 1992; Haberman 1995). In a book describing beliefs and practices of teachers successful with students from poverty, Haberman writes about future teachers that misconceptions about why people are poor "are as common among future teachers as in the population at large. Pre-service students' typical explanations of poverty include the full range of stereotypes: the poor are stupid, lazy, without initiative, and lacking in moral responsibility for themselves and their families" (1995, 50–51).

How a person understands the causes of poverty is a barometer of attitudes toward families and children living in poverty. Ryan, a psychologist and social scientist, stated unequivocally that "the ideology of Blaming the Victim so distorts and disorients the thinking of the average concerned citizen that it becomes a primary barrier to effective social change" (1971, xv). *Blaming the victim* has taken two forms, according to Ryan, who popularized the term. First was what he labels the old-fashioned conservative belief system that put an emphasis on intrinsic or even hereditary defects of one sort or another as the causes of poverty, dismissing victims of poverty "as inferior, genetically defective, or morally unfit" (7). A newer approach looks at the contribution of what is called a culture of poverty, or the environment, and makes the stigma of poverty "an acquired stigma, a stigma of social, rather than genetic, origin" (7). No matter which approach, the end result is that the problem is seen as within the victim; therefore, programs to address poverty focus on changing in some way the person or the behaviors of the person who is poor.

The poor present problems to those of us living outside the immediate ravages of poverty, so we tend to address causes of poverty as external to ourselves rather than seeing ourselves or society as causes. We can remain comfortably distant. Ryan states, "The typical Victim Blamer is a middle-class person who is doing reasonably well in a material way; he has a good job, a good income, a good house, a good car. Basically, he likes the social system pretty much as it is, as least in broad outline" (1971, 26). Yet many middle-class persons espouse humanitarian beliefs and contribute in many ways to the services and charities that serve the poor. Says Ryan, "They cannot bring themselves to attack the system that has been so good to them, but they want so badly to be helpful to the victims of racism and economic injustice" (27). In fact, blaming the victim has provided for millions a way out of this moral dilemma created in the confrontation of self-interest with humanitarianism. If we simply blame the victim, we do not have to look at the cruelties of either our economic system or our public policies, or in Ryan's words, "those who buy this solution with a sigh of relief are inevitably blinding themselves to the basic causes of the problems being addressed" (1971, 28).

Wilson (1996) clarifies beyond doubt how the economic system and public policy decisions have created the world of what he calls the new urban poor. He defines the new urban poverty to mean those "poor, segregated neighborhoods in which a substantial majority of individual adults are either unemployed or have dropped out of the labor force altogether" (19). Based on twenty-five years of sociological studies focused on Chicago's South Side neighborhoods, Wilson concludes, "Many of today's problems in the inner-city ghetto neighborhoods—crime, family dissolution, welfare, low levels of social organization, and so on—are fundamentally a consequence of the disappearance of work" (xiii). The book traces the evolution of Chicago's ghetto, "the emergence of concentrated and persistent joblessness and its crippling effects on neighborhoods, families, and individuals" (17).

The Chicago story repeated itself in major urban areas throughout the country as city after city lost its manufacturing jobs. Deepening poverty has been the consequence. "In 1959, less than one-third of the poverty population in the United Stated lived in metropolitan central cities. By 1991, the central cities included close to half of the nation's poor," Wilson (1996, 11) wrote. For example, Chicago lost 60 percent of its manufacturing jobs between 1967 and 1987 due to technological advances, movement of work to the suburbs, and the internationalization of production. Whites and blacks who could afford to moved to the suburbs where the jobs were, but many poor blacks stayed behind. The contribution of public policy decisions to the concentration of poverty in urban centers included, to name only a few, government withholding of mortgage capital from urban neighborhoods, federal transportation and highway policies, suburban resistance to integration by class and construction of public housing, urban renewal policies, and government toleration of industry practices that undermined worker security through reducing benefits and increasing reliance on involuntary part-time employment of temporary workers in all kinds of jobs. Jobs and wages declined at the same time that employment opportunities and people moved to the suburbs.

The economic recession of the 1980s deepened poverty for the urban poor and cities lost much federal support for basic urban programs. Additionally, "targeted programs for the poor in the United States [did] not even begin to address inequities in the social class system" (Wilson 1996, 156). He contrasts U.S. public policy initiatives with those in Europe where citizens are presumed to have social rights to decent housing, medical care, economic security, and employment. He understands the differences in approach to reveal differences in underlying beliefs and attitudes about the causes of poverty. Speaking of the United States, Wilson wrote, "Beliefs that associate joblessness and poverty with individual shortcomings do not generate strong support for social programs intended to end inequality" (159). According to recurring polls, citizens in European countries consistently and by a wide margin "favored structural explanations over individual explanations for the causes of poverty" (160), whereas results of such surveys in the United States are the opposite.

A BRIEF HISTORY OF DEFICIT THINKING

Deficit thinking about members of minority groups has been around for at least a century. Menchaca (1997) traces ideas of genetic inferiority of people of color back to the arrival of the Pilgrims in 1620, who brought with them an attitude of superiority to the Native Americans coupled with religious beliefs common among Europeans. For example, "A common opinion was that the dark races were descendants of the devil" (15). The intersection of religious beliefs and economic interest led to extensive proselytizing and land displacement of Native Americans. By the late 1600s, Great Britain was sending large numbers of African slaves to the colonies. "In America, the racial belief that Africans were not human beings and their enslavement was not against God's will was a popular argument used to condone slavery" (16). Debate about whether the human races belonged to different species was active at some level until 1859 when Charles Darwin argued "that all the races were of a modern human stock and had gradually, and in one line, evolved from a common origin" (30). Previously, Menchaca explained, according to missionaries, "Africans and American Indians were viewed as savages whose cultural environment has prevented them from cognitively developing in the same manner as Caucasians" (17). After the Civil War there were basically two sides to the academic debate about racial superiority: "On one side were the craniologists and social Darwinists who espoused a far-right white supremacy racist discourse and on the other side were historians who presented a moderate racist position" (34). In spite of the Emancipation Proclamation, by the 1870s, the alleged cultural and intellectual inferiority of African Americans was routinely used to justify many varieties of discrimination and poor treatment, including slavery. Poor whites were also considered to be intellectually inferior, but they did not suffer the same treatment as African Americans and Native Americans.

The earliest manifestations of deficit thinking in education contained expressions of both genetic and cultural inferiority. According to Valencia, "The genetic pathology model of deficit thinking—which contends that inferiority is transmitted by the genetic code—held currency from about 1890 to 1930" (1997, 41). Intelligence testing arrived under its influence, and led to curriculum differentiation based on perceived measured intelligence. In 1923 in California, the Oakland schools became the first district to adopt a "systemwide program of mass intelligence testing for homogeneous groupings" (75–76). In the 1920s, vocational education developed quickly as an alternative for those students seen as unlikely by virtue of IQ to succeed in a more academic curriculum. These developments altered the structure of opportunity in schools. The *genetic pathology* movement experienced a decline in the 1930s and 1940s, at first partly influenced by the Depression, when many became poor, and then in the backlash against the Nazi atrocities. Deficit thinking as an explanation for the achievement gap did not go away but assumed another form, influenced by anthropology and the writings of Oscar Lewis, an anthropologist who developed the *culture of poverty* concept. "He emphasized that people living in poverty tend to create a unique, self-sustaining life-style or way of life marked by a host of negative values, norms and social practices" (Foley 1997, 115). Interestingly, Lewis wrote in 1965, "The culture of poverty was found in capitalist countries only" (Foley 1997, 116).

After the 1954 Supreme Court decision officially ended segregation in schools, deficit thinking was typically expressed as *cultural deprivation*, a psychological model that was an outgrowth of the anthropological culture of poverty explanation. Also known as the *cultural disadvantagement* model, it blamed the family for the transmission of deficiencies to children. These deficiencies were thought to range from linguistic and cognitive impairment to "pathogenic personality characteristics" that impeded ability to learn (Pearl 1997a, 133). Other cultural explanations used to explain differences in school achievement were inadequate socialization and accumulated environmental deficits. These cultural theories were the basis of educational and social policy that emerged with compensatory education and the War on Poverty in the 1960s. The theories still have credibility. "Culture reemerges as a major focus in recent years as part of interest in diversity and an emphasis on multicultural/bilingual education with 'deficit' transmogrified into 'difference'" (Pearl 1997a, 137). Today, according to Pearl, the concepts of difference and deficit coexist. Valencia (1997) believes:

> Although the deficit thinking model is held in disrepute by many contemporary behavioral and social scientists, there is mounting evidence that deficit thinking is experiencing a resurgence in current educational thought and practice. . . . The popular "at-risk" construct, now entrenched in educational circles, views poor and working-class children and their families (typically of color) as being predominantly responsible for school failure, while frequently holding structural inequality blameless. (xi)

INFLUENCING BELIEFS AND ATTITUDES ABOUT FAMILIES LIVING IN POVERTY

Our case studies and other research suggest strongly that high-performing, high-poverty schools are led and staffed by educators who believe that all children can learn at high levels. We know, however, that many high-poverty schools are low performing and that many educators participate in deficit thinking about the children and their families. Regardless of whether an educator is influenced by the genetic or cultural form, beliefs and attitudes associated with deficit thinking are negative and do not encourage the effort required to successfully teach children living in poverty. The challenge for a principal is to influence faculty and staff to abandon deficit thinking and embrace the belief that all children can learn at high levels, that all children have enormous potential and promise. Beliefs, attitudes, and opinions can change. Contemporary leadership theorist Heifetz (1994) offers ideas about leadership and growth that can help principals bring about the adaptive changes that involve values, beliefs, and behavior. Goodman's (2001) work about how to develop support for multiculturalism suggests both a theoretical foundation and practical steps for bringing about attitude change. Wheatley (2002) reminds us of the power of conversation to bring about change.

A Leadership Theory

Heifetz (1994) understands that leadership is not about providing easy answers. He provides an analysis of leadership as the promotion of adaptive work, a view that emerged from his training and work as a psychiatrist as well as his years of teaching leadership at Harvard's Kennedy School of Government. "Mobilizing people to tackle tough problems" is the image he builds in elaborating leadership tasks (15). He conceives of leadership as an activity that makes possible adaptive work.

> Adaptive work consists of the learning required to address conflicts in the values people hold, or to diminish the gap between the values people stand for and the reality they face. Adaptive work requires a change in values, beliefs, or behavior. The exposure and orchestration of conflict—internal contradictions—within individuals and constituencies provide the leverage for mobilizing people to learn new ways. (22)

Specifically, Heifetz writes, "Tackling tough problems—problems that often require an evolution of values—is the end of leadership; getting that work done is its essence" (26).

What his theory means for principals is that leading is about asking the tough questions that might, for example, reveal to individuals the gaps between their espoused beliefs in the ability of every child to learn and their teaching practices. Heifetz describes learning as requiring people to interpret problem situations differently. Learning will be required for many educators to interpret learning problems as school failures instead of blaming the victims. Using Heifetz's terminology, blaming the victim is a form of work avoidance on the part of educators. Work avoidance, often unconscious, results from the natural resistance of people to the distress and hard work of adaptive change, which to use the example of working more successfully with low-income students might require changes in beliefs and teaching practices. When persons experience the "uncentering" of hard problems, they often adopt defensive routines to avoid the challenge of adaptive work. Such work avoidance can take many forms: "holding onto past assumptions, blaming authority, scapegoating, externalizing the enemy, denying the problem, jumping to conclusions, or finding a distracting issue may restore stability and feel less stressful than facing and taking responsibility for a complex challenge" (37).

Principals successful in promoting attitude change can ask the tough questions and are also able to create holding environments that allow and support the developmental learning required. A holding environment is created when a leader contains the stresses of adaptive work as much as possible by being supportive of persons at all stages of growth. Creating a holding environment implies trust. Heifetz understands trust to be "a matter of predictability along two dimensions: values and skills" (107). Listening with empathy, sequencing, pacing, framing issues, and directing attention are all valuable leadership skills that support adaptive change. Heifetz believes that "over time, a community can become familiar with adaptive work, its pain and its profit" (129). In summary, he defines leadership as teaching: "Leadership is a special sort of education in which the teacher raises problems, questions, options, interpretations, and perspectives, often without answers, gauging all the while when to push through and when to hold steady" (244–45).

Applying his leadership ideas to issues of attitudes toward poverty, we see the potential for attitude change. Effective principals in high-poverty schools address the inconsistencies of teachers who treat children living in poverty differently from other children. They must work relentlessly to eliminate the work avoidance signified by a "blaming the victim" mentality. By building trusting relationships, effective principals create holding environments that facilitate the developmental steps required for significant attitudinal or behavioral change.

Bryk and Schneider (2002) also emphasize the importance of relational trust to academic achievement in high-poverty urban schools. Based on their research about successful high-poverty Chicago schools, they write, "The personal dynamics among teachers, students, and their parents, for example, influence whether students regularly attend school and sustain efforts on the difficult tasks of learning" (5). They describe relational trust as an organizational property based on congruence of a principal's "beliefs and observed behavior" (22). Relational trust grows when a principal expresses personal regard or care for individuals within the school community.

A Theory about Attitude Change

Goodman (2001) addresses from a theoretical perspective how people from privileged groups can be educated to support social justice. This process of education combines approaches to increase empathy, engage moral principles and spiritual values, and appeal to self-interest. "Being empathic, or taking the perspective of another person and imagining how that person is affected by his or her plight, can be useful for promoting more positive attitudes and inspiring action," Goodman writes (126). Empathy can be developed cognitively through information as well as affectively through personal experience with others different from ourselves. Either of these approaches counteracts the depersonalization and dehumanization often accorded to families living in poverty. Greater knowledge of the realities of poverty can provoke both the personal and sympathetic distress likely to generate caring actions. In Goodman's words, "Once we have empathized and feel some kind of empathic or sympathetic distress, we have to decide what to do about it" (129). Approaches can include exposing people to other life experiences "through books, movies, panels, and personal testimony" (144).

The second approach, appealing to moral principles and spiritual values, can invoke either the ethic of care or the ethic of justice, or both. Taken seriously, either can provide a powerful motivation to try to right the wrongs of an unjust society. Goodman believes that "despite their many differences, most religious or spiritual belief systems share a common mandate to care for those less fortunate and to treat people humanely" (2001, 134), so the ethic of care is ingrained in the religious beliefs of many persons. For the privileged to take issues of justice seriously is more complex. As a first step, education about the systemic inequity that supports poverty must be offered. Systemic economic injustice must be understood conceptually before the facts of living in poverty in the richest country in the world can be grasped as injustice. If persons gather personal stories, and otherwise confront the realities of poverty, perhaps through books such as Kozol's (1995) *Amazing Grace: The Lives of Children and the Conscience of a Nation*, then an in-depth understanding of the injustice of systemic poverty can be reached. Information and understanding reduce the tendency to blame the victim. Care and justice work together. "As a human activity, justice-making is forged or fired by the passion of caring. Caring clearly precedes justice; justice is born from caring. The order is not usually reversed. When we care, we act, become angry with injustice and seek remedies" (Lyman 2000, 151). Goodman (2001) summarizes this approach in these words: "By invoking moral principles and spiritual values, people can be motivated to live up to and according to one's values and to right what they perceive as a wrong" (151).

Finally, the third approach, self-interest, is not necessarily about selfishness. The continuum of self-interest ranges from a focus on *me* to the interdependence of *us*. Certainly a strong argument can be made for the necessity of educational success for the children of the have-nots of the country. Their success is not only desirable from the point of view of economics but is a factor that can contribute immeasurably to giving us a good society, one in which we can all be proud to live. Both short-term and long-term self-interest suggest that as a society we need to alleviate the dire poverty affecting too many children. Goodman (2001) recommends that educators utilize a combination of these potential motivators—empathy, moral principles and spiritual values, and self-interest—to influence the privileged to support social justice goals, such as the closing of the achievement gap.

The Power of Conversation

Wheatley (2002) advocates turning to the power of conversation as a way to bring about changes in the world. "Human conversation is the most ancient and easiest way to cultivate the conditions for change—personal change, community and organizational change, planetary change," she writes (3). She sees conversation as a process through which we "evoke more goodness from one another" (8). The achievement gap and deficit thinking are surely two of the most intractable problems faced by the educational community. Could we begin to approach these anew by talking with one another, sharing our experiences, becoming more aware of our own prejudicial beliefs and attitudes, truly listening to all persons involved in and affected by the achievement gap? Wheatley writes, "Over the years, I've noticed that many of us harbor negative beliefs about each other. Or we believe that there's nothing we can do to make a difference. Or that things are so crazy that we have to look out for ourselves. With these beliefs, we cannot turn to one another. We won't engage together for the work that needs to be done" (18).

Her book contains guidelines for hosting a good conversation. A good conversation requires the willingness to be disturbed, to admit that we don't know, that we are confused. Speaking specifically about the power of conversation, Wheatley writes, "To advocate human conversation as the means to restore hope to the future is as simple as I can get. But I've seen that there is no more powerful way to initiate significant change than to convene a conversation. When a community of people discovers that they share a concern, change begins. There is no power equal to a community discovering what it cares about" (22). If charity, meaning a spirit of love, begins at home, then certainly educational conversations should begin first *at home*, among the faculty and staff of any school truly wanting high-level learning for all students. Such a conversation would not be a one-time thing. Such a conversation would explore ideas and beliefs of each person about the *why* of now, as well as the *way* to the possible future. Eventually, principals in high-poverty schools can include students, parents, and community members in such conversations. The persistence of both the achievement gap and deficit thinking are genuine educational emergencies calling for action, for the courage of genuine conversation.

Summary

Changing beliefs and attitudes is a slow process. Principals can appeal to moral principles and spiritual values by asking provocative questions that expose the gaps between beliefs and practices at both classroom and school levels. Empathy can develop when teachers make home visits and gather more information by undertaking action research, investigating community agencies that serve the poor, and getting to know the children and their family members. Finally, change happens when educators understand that change is in their own best interests. A new vision of what a teaching day might be like could happen for some teachers through visiting schools where children living in poverty are succeeding at a high level. For other teachers, rigorous self-evaluation of their own teaching practices and results could lead to understanding that change might be in their own best interest as professionals. Perhaps for others the best practice of all would be meaningful and frequent conversations.

BELIEFS AND ATTITUDES ABOUT POVERTY AT HARRISON AND NEWFIELD SCHOOLS

To understand more deeply the dynamics of the two successful schools in our case studies, we explored through a written survey the beliefs and attitudes of the Harrison and Newfield faculty and staff members toward poverty, asking them not only about their attitudes but also their perceptions of attitudes of other educators. We were interested in exploring our assumption that different attitudes toward poverty exist in schools where children from low-income families are learning and achieving at high levels. Responses were received from thirty-six persons divided between the two schools.

Responses to the question "What are your attitudes and beliefs about poverty?" elicited a range of answers. Some chose to comment on poverty's causes or to define poverty. For example, one person wrote, "Poverty includes more than lack of money. Poverty may include a lack of role models and emotional support." Another wrote, "After multi-generations in poverty a learned helplessness seems to permeate. A culture of language and attitude runs through people of poverty." Several referred to the impact of generational poverty and appreciated that this life experience challenges resiliency, but is not impossible to overcome. Generally, a strong theme in the answers was that families *can* rise above their circumstances and create better lives for themselves and their children. Only a few expressed blame toward the families; more were empathetic with their circumstances. One person wrote, "Poverty can happen to anyone." These teachers seemed to understand how the culture and society contribute toward keeping large numbers of people in poverty. They seemed to understand that poverty might affect the way children learn, but that the children are quite capable of learning. In the words of one teacher, "They can learn just as well as other children can learn." Another person wrote, "It is the responsibility of teachers in poverty-stricken areas to ensure all students have an equal chance to succeed." Generally, at least half of the responses expressed a positive attitude toward families and children living in poverty, with the next largest category of responses neutral or explanatory, and only a few expressing negativity.

The responses to the second question, "What do you think are educators' attitudes and beliefs about poverty?," were interesting. A small minority expressed the belief that many educators do not feel poor students can learn. For example, one person wrote, "A lot of educators believe that since they come from such poor conditions that they are not capable of succeeding in school." Others wrote of how educators in other schools do not understand poverty, writing that they "treat it as ignorance or some sort of disease. Just about the same way that they think of minorities." A majority of respondents' views described a polarity with teachers falling into one of two categories: either that educators were ignorant or discouraged, or that educators viewed helping poor children learn as a mission. For example, one person wrote, "I think there are some educators who would not want to teach children in poverty or go into a school like ours. On the other hand some would want to do this, finding it rewarding." Still another person wrote, "Some educators believe that poverty means low income, low self-esteem, and behavior problems. Other educators believe that it is their destiny to help children successfully beat the repeated cycle of poverty." A few, however, commented directly that beliefs of those at other schools tended toward negativity because of a lack of understanding and experience. For example, "We are willing to look at the families in poverty and give them the same or more opportunities to become productive citizens. I tend to believe that other educators stereotype students from poverty in ways that are not justified."

The third survey question directly asked respondents to comment on other educators' beliefs about the potential of the children for academic achievement: "What do you think educators believe regarding children who live in poverty and educational achievement?" Approximately half wrote that other educators believe poverty means poor achievement. For example, one person wrote, "They have low expectations and teach the children according to that belief." Several others also addressed the prevalence of lowered expectations. For example, one wrote, "They believe that students in poverty will not achieve in school and that they will just drop out." Another expressed hopelessness in these words, "I think that a large percentage of educators believe that poverty stricken children will continue to live in poverty regardless of their educational/teaching efforts." On the other hand, half of those surveyed described their own beliefs and made positive statements about the learning potential of the children, including how as teachers they could help learning happen. For example, one person wrote, "Every child is capable of academic achievement. Children in poverty need more concrete hands-on learning within a stable environment." One comment displayed rich understanding: "Many times children who come from poverty areas are further behind in all academic areas, especially socially. But just because a child comes from a poverty home does not mean that the child is not smart or teachable. These children need a little more assistance to get the stimulation and experiences they were not able to get at home." A final example speaks to the task of helping students believe they can succeed. The person wrote, "Educators must believe that children in poverty can succeed. Making the child believe in himself and his success in life and education can be more difficult, but not impossible." A few comments implied or specifically addressed the difference between beliefs of other educators and the beliefs of persons at their schools. For example, one person wrote, "Those educators who work and teach in areas of poverty know that these children can and will often learn what is necessary for them to learn. They can achieve above and beyond if an educator puts forth the effort for them to achieve that goal. Some educators may believe children of poverty can't learn above a certain limit, but those are the ones not familiar with them."

In the two schools we studied, productive beliefs and attitudes regarding the children and their potential prevailed. On the whole, the responses to these three questions suggest a group of persons with generally positive attitudes toward working with poor children and their families, toward their potential for success in learning and life. As a group, they recognize that their perspectives may not be typical, and acknowledge the complexity of working with children and families in poverty. Half believe that other educators generally equate poverty with low expectations and poor achievement. Generally, their written comments imply what we contend, that educators who understand the complexity of poverty have different attitudes from the norm and that those more-positive beliefs and attitudes are a factor in their success as educators of children living in poverty.

CHALLENGES AND REWARDS FOR
EDUCATORS IN HIGH-POVERTY SCHOOLS

Interview responses of the Harrison and Newfield faculty and staff provide an overview of the challenges and rewards experienced by educators in high-poverty schools. The challenges are clear. The two biggest challenges were working with the parents and working with the discipline/behavior problems and issues of the children. They were realistic about the challenging parents, many of whom either do not seem to value education or had bad school experiences themselves and so are mistrustful of educators. One mentioned the value of knowing that the principal was strong and "would intervene to support us." In addition to interventions, another teacher valued knowing "if I have a difficult time with a parent, I can come to her and gain some strength." An equal number of comments about discipline and behavior problems and issues ranged from the difficulty of understanding the behaviors to the difficulty of dealing with the behaviors. One explained, "Discipline was really difficult because I did not know what they were thinking or why they were doing what they were doing. I did not know how to react to that then and I did not know what would be the best way to diffuse a situation." Another said about behaviors, "The inexplicability is the hard part. There are times when there is no explanation on why a child is disobedient, disrespectful, and violent." Underlying these behavior challenges is what the next largest group identified as the different reality of the children. One teacher elaborated in these words, "They have so many things going on in their minds and sometimes I feel that it is difficult for them to think about learning. Sometimes they need to tell me first what is worrying them before we can start the lessons. You have to start with how they feel, what is going on." Another said, "There are some things that the children say or do and I wonder where they would come up with that at this young age." Two other challenges mentioned by only a few were the language deficits of the children and that there is "never enough time" to do everything a teacher wants.

On the other hand, the rewards were equally clear. One of the categories was seeing families become successful. One person said, "To see a family become a success story" was his greatest reward. Another spoke of making a difference for families. A third talked about working with families as a way of giving back to the community, about how she enjoyed seeing adults achieve. In another category were remarks about the rewards of "learning every day" that the school offered to each of them as staff members. One talked of how the children taught her things. A new teacher said, "I have learned so much, I learn every day still. I learn so much about myself, my limits, how I handle stress."

The largest number framed the rewards in terms of the learning of the children, and quality of relationships with the children and others in the school. The learning of the children was mentioned in terms of achievement test scores, but more importantly in terms of the rewards of how children "are able to do numerous things they could not do when they walked into the classroom." Several mentioned the joy of seeing a child learn to read and write. One elaborated about the thrill of seeing emotional learning happen. She said, "To see a child go from just being so angry that they can't do anything to turning themselves around, not necessarily because of anything I have said or done, but just seeing that change is really rewarding to me too." One person elaborated on the special quality of the school that grows out of the goodness of the children. "When I started I knew most of these kids had very little to be cheerful about, had very little reason to be trusting and happy, but all the while there has been this underlying goodness about the place. You have probably had some child ask you if you needed any help, or if you knew where you were going. There are just so many tiny miracles here." Another mentioned how loving the children are, still another cited "the smiles and hugs from the children." One commented on the environment from an even broader perspective when she said she found rewarding that the children are being taken care of and loved. Another stated the rewards in terms of being needed by the children: "That is a huge reward, knowing that if I were gone a day, they'd know it and would miss me, and have a million questions for me the next day."

The challenges express the frustration of professionals working in a demanding environment. The rewards are expressions of hope and satisfaction born of hard work and positive attitudes toward children and their potential. The rewards of working with children from low-income families can be enormous when educators believe in the ability of the children and their promise, put themselves at risk through innovative teaching, offer persistent encouragement, maintain high expectations, demonstrate regard for the family and circumstances of each child, display above-and-beyond effort, and never give up.

CONCLUSIONS

We are not alone in viewing deficit thinking on the part of educators as a significant contributor to the achievement gap (Haberman 1995, 1999; Jackson 2003; Quint 1994; Reyes, Scribner, and Scribner 1999; Riester, Pursch, and Skrla 2002; Scheurich 1998; Shields 2003; Valencia 1997; Valverde and Scribner 2001; Wagstaff and Fusarelli 1995). A principal aptly describes the reality of deficit thinking in too many schools:

> Few Americans believe that all children *can* learn at high levels. Most believe that children are born (as Jeff Howard puts it) very smart, sorta smart, and kinda dumb. Most educators doubt that it is possible to change this basic endowment no matter how effective a learning experience they provide. By and large, teachers work hard, get unequal results (with some students not making it), and do not see that as a reflection on their work. Even fewer teachers believe that all children *should* learn at high levels. There is a deep-seated attitude that students get the grades they deserve. (Marshall 1996, 307)

Haberman's (1995, 1999) conclusions from research on teachers and principals who successfully serve children in poverty also support the importance of educators' attitudes to students' learning. Speaking of teachers generally, as a result of inadequate teacher preparation, Haberman contends that new teachers especially view children of poverty as abnormal or deficient. "Children and youth in poverty face teachers who begin with the assumption that most of them should not be there," he writes (1995, 4). On the other hand, those he calls *star* teachers expect a diverse range of achievement, build personal relationships with children around the tasks of learning rather than behavior issues, and believe that most parents care about their children. "Star teachers do not blame parents"; rather they communicate with respect and build cooperation (11). The successful teachers "not only believe that all children in poverty can learn, but that they should learn as much as possible in the widest possible range of subjects" (16–17). He presents fifteen functions or teaching strategies of star teachers as outgrowths of their belief in learning as natural. The first—and in many ways, most important—of these characteristics is the persistence that reveals "the deep and abiding beliefs that stars hold about the nature of children in poverty and their potential" (21). They establish close and supportive relationships with most of the children they teach

(54), and take the time to get to know the individual situations of their students so they can make learning more relevant. Caring is part of their professionalism and is extended to children, even when they seem unlovable. They are organized, admit mistakes, have stamina, and believe that effort creates success for themselves as well as the children and youth they serve. Haberman emphasizes what he called their "gentle teaching" (1995, 86) as a conscious contrast to the violence in the lives of many of the children. They will not resort to measures of control in order to reach children, but rely on the intrinsic value of learning and their own abilities to teach.

In focusing on star principals, Haberman (1999) is even more explicit about the link between belief and successful practices. He writes, "The ideology and the behaviors are interwoven: they are of a piece. The connection between what star principals do and how they think about what they do cannot be broken" (x). In fact, he states, "this ideology is a value-laden system of beliefs *caught* and developed by life experiences rather than *taught* in graduate courses in school administration" (xi). Haberman views a person's attitude toward explaining difficulties in schools' successes with children of poverty as predictive of his or her ability to be a successful principal. Those who blame the victim tend to rationalize their own inactions and become complacent, he argues. We agree with Haberman's (1999) statement that principals need to take responsibility for educating staff members:

> The essential job of the principal in implementing a belief in students' potential is to move teachers from blaming the victim to assuming accountability for what and how much children can learn. For the principal to accomplish this incredibly difficult task, he or she must personally believe in students' potential. If the principal believes effort . . . is the best explanation of success in school, then he or she may be able to change resistant teachers. However, if the principal believes in the ability paradigm and that the forces of poverty cannot be overcome by improving schools, then he or she becomes the spokesperson and leader of faculty burnouts. (38)

Haberman views persistence as important for principals as well as teachers, calling it a characteristic that predicts a principal's ability to lead a school where learning goals are met for all students. He encourages democratic decision making and advocates a willingness to admit fallibility. He emphasizes that in situations of urban poverty working with three principles will

create successful schools. These principles are "unity of purpose, team building, and commitment to task" (31). Haberman's work (1995, 1999) supports
our observations and our emphasis on positive beliefs and attitudes as fundamental to high-performing, high-poverty schools.

Achievement is not supported in schools where educators do not believe
in the ability of children from low-income minority homes to learn at high
levels. All children need encouragement, particularly those struggling with
issues of poverty. Pearl writes, "It is the *differential* encouragements main-
tained by statute, enacted by policy and informally practiced by classroom
teachers and administrators that help to perpetuate deficit thinking. . . . Students with 'deficits' are not encouraged to survive the obstacle course, as
they see no reason to invest in schools" (1997b, 213–216).

Prejudices and deficit thinking about the poor and members of minority groups persist in America. Educators are not immune from the widespread stereotypes about the lower intelligence of African Americans and
other persons of color. Interestingly, in the United States, explanations
given for the low achievement of minority children living in poverty echo
the typical beliefs about causes of poverty. Low achievement and causes
of poverty are both understood by many people to result from deficiencies
of individual students and their families. Learning problems and poverty
are viewed as genetic problems or as having arisen from cultural influences. The achievement gap is growing and understanding the complexity
of poverty and its effects on children and their families has not been a priority for educators, teachers, or administrators.

As a result of a national study of educational leadership programs, we
found that understanding the complexity of poverty is not an emphasis in
the vast majority of programs (Lyman and Villani 2002). Whereas a third
of the respondents (department chairs) viewed understanding poverty as
extremely important to effective leadership, they perceived that only 11.6
percent of their faculty members would agree (261–262). This low per-
ception of the importance of understanding the complexity of poverty is
substantiated by its low emphasis in brochure and catalog descriptions of
programs, class activities, and in performance expectations and compe-
tencies for graduates (262–264).

Clearly, teacher education and educational leadership programs do not
assist teachers and leaders in understanding the poverty system. Until this
occurs, stereotypical attitudes will contribute to maintaining the achieve-

ment gap. When principals are willing to grapple with how beliefs and attitudes about poverty converge with prejudicial beliefs and attitudes about racial and ethnic minority children, thereby affecting teachers' efforts and nonverbal messages to children and their parents, then students' levels of learning and achievement will increase. Our contention is that when principals understand the critical importance of educating beliefs and attitudes within a school, they will take action to do so.

Chapter Seven

Making a Difference

School can be a place of peril when educators remain uninformed and unenlightened about the complexities of poverty. Beliefs, attitudes, and limited knowledge regarding poverty are a threat to the academic achievement, self-esteem, and opportunities available to children living in low-income families. Cottle writes, "At a very young age children begin to recognize that they are being put at peril for no reason other than that their skin is dark or that they are poor" (2001, 12). He raises this question about our society, "What can be said about a culture that permits children to live without adequate shelter or go malnourished for years?" (3). In the same spirit of moral outrage, we, the authors, ask what can be said about an educational system that *allows* children who live in poverty to fail academically and treats them as if there were a causal relationship existing between being poor and ability to learn? Where are the leaders with knowledge and commitment to build school communities that support the academic, personal, and social development of *all* students? What is required for leaders in high-poverty schools to make a difference in the achievement and opportunities of children from low-income families? We began the research that led to this book to explore these and other questions. We believe that powerful leadership in high-poverty schools begins conceptually with questioning current paradigms and dropping what Barth (1990) has called the burden of presumed competence. Heifetz expresses this wisdom in these words, "One may lead perhaps with no more than a question in hand" (1994, 276). We end the book by posing questions that beg for continued exploration, emphasizing the need for change, and highlighting the challenges of social justice leadership.

THE QUESTIONS

As leaders, both Aurthur Perkins and Carmen Perez-Dickson take a relational approach, get things done, have high expectations, are dedicated and passionate role models, and are visible in giving above-and-beyond effort within their school communities. They provide instructive models, but their ways of leading grow out of their backgrounds and are uniquely suited to the contexts of their respective schools. Each does, however, serve as a powerful *mirror* within which to examine oneself as a leader. The goal of self-reflection as a leader is deeper insight into one's own beliefs, attitudes, and practices. Self-reflection puts one on a path toward elimination of unconscious prejudices, behavioral inconsistencies, and internal contradictions. The path ends in authenticity. Authentic leaders whose actions match their beliefs make a difference. As Bolman and Deal state so eloquently, "The essence of leadership is not giving things or even providing visions. It is offering oneself and one's spirit" (1995, 102). The best leadership practices for high-poverty schools cannot be reduced to a list or a formula. Leadership that makes a difference is always contextual and grows out of individual strengths. Rather than answers, we offer and discuss five questions for continuing reflection:

- What does the research about successful high-poverty schools say and what do we need to know more about?
- How can belief in the ability and promise of the children be cultivated?
- How can professional development contribute to successful high-poverty schools?
- How can collective leadership be developed in a school?
- How are meaningful partnerships created with families and the community?

Question One

What does the research say about successful high-poverty schools and what do we need to know more about?

A major recurrent finding in the research about beliefs of principals in successful high-poverty schools is that the children flourish and learn when a principal and teachers believe in their abilities. They need a principal and teachers who value and care about them and their families. Two other essential components are family-centered schools and professional development to support the work of the teachers. Our comparative analysis of strategies of principals in successful high-poverty schools identified issues associated with teacher quality, goals, working with parents, testing and monitoring, and curriculum design. A curriculum aligned with state and national standards provides a foundation for learning and achievement. Only a partial compilation of available sources, our book nevertheless provides an entry point into the research about successful high-poverty schools. Informed leadership means attending conferences, reading professional journals, and being aware of promising new practices. With knowledge of important research findings comes the responsibility to implement research-based practices.

An aspect of the research that we have not explored in this book is the literature about effective teaching practices in high-poverty schools. In urban schools, a recurring theme is the importance of caring teachers who believe in the worth and learning ability of their students. In particular, principals in schools where the majority of students are from minority groups need to know the literature about effective teaching practices for students of color. Principals need to know, for example, the work of Delpit (1995), Ladson-Billings (1994, 2001), Gay (2000), Murrell (2002), and Scribner and Reyes (1999). Each of these scholars offers unique but related insights. Ladson-Billings reminds us, "most teachers have little or no genuine experience with cultures different from their own" (2001, 78). She advocates learning to develop cultural competence, so that teaching will foster the ability of students to grow in understanding and respect of their own cultures. Her work focuses on improving the school experiences and academic achievement of African American children through *culturally relevant* teaching. She writes, "No challenge has been more daunting than that of improving the academic achievement of African American students. Burdened with a history that includes the denial of education, separate and unequal education, and relegation to unsafe, substandard inner-city schools, the quest for quality education remains an elusive dream for the African American community" (1994, ix). Gay argues, "a very different pedagogical paradigm is needed to improve the performance of underachieving students from various ethnic groups—one that teaches *to and through* their personal and cultural strengths, their intellectual capabilities, and their prior accomplishments" (2000, 24). Her book advances such a paradigm, which she calls *culturally responsive* teaching.

Delpit's work (1995) asks us to understand that African American children are strongly bonded to both family and the larger collective community group. She writes and speaks eloquently about teaching that touches and liberates the spirit of the children. She calls on teachers to be seed planters, humanitarians, and teachers of the spirit. She helps us understand the conflicts that can emerge in a classroom because of ignorance, prejudices, cultural misunderstandings, and differences in language dialects, to name a few. Delpit reminds us, "If we do not have some knowledge of children's lives outside of the realms of paper-and-pencil work, and even outside of their classrooms, then we cannot know their strengths" (173). Her book ends with these powerful words: "If we are to successfully educate all of our children, we must work to remove the blinders built of stereotypes, monocultural instructional methodologies, ignorance, social distance, biased research, and racism. We must work to destroy those blinders so that it is possible to really see, to really know the students we must teach" (182). Addressing those of us seeking better educational experiences for poor children and children of color, Delpit writes, "The answers, I believe, lie not in a proliferation of new reform programs but in some basic understandings of who we are and how we are connected to and disconnected from one another" (xv). At some level, all teachers can be said to educate other people's children; but if we remain ignorant about or do not value the cultures of those we teach, we cannot connect with them. That lack of connection will certainly complicate and can altogether block learning and achievement.

Murrell offers a vision for building a community of African American achievement through teachers who can connect students "with their own heritage and legacy of achievement as a definition of what it means to be African American in the United States" (2002, 123). He presents an instructional theory for integrating historical, cultural, political, and developmental aspects of African American experience, calling the theory *African-centered pedagogy*. His work incorporates five existing frameworks:

- Communities of learning, communities of caring
- Culturally responsive, culturally synchronous, culturally relevant teaching
- Teaching for understanding, constructivist teaching

- Situated learning theory
- Cultural communities as ecosocial systems for identity development (xii–xiii)

Scribner and Reyes (1999) provide a good resource for understanding culturally responsive pedagogy for Hispanic students. They believe "culturally responsive pedagogy is required for students to succeed in a high-performing learning community for Hispanic students" (199). They articulate the components of such pedagogy as follows:

- Teachers believe every student has the ability to achieve, and they communicate this belief to students, parents, and colleagues.
- Teachers provide a caring environment in which students are viewed as the most valuable resources of the school.
- Teachers empower their students, providing opportunities for experimentation, innovation, discovery, and problem solving.
- Teachers make use of two-way "instructional conversations" with students that encourage goal-directed activity and the use of higher-order thinking skills on the part of students.
- Teachers use students' funds of knowledge as the basis of their instructional strategies. (200–3)

They conclude, in summary, that a key to high-performing Hispanic schools is *relevance* of the learning environment to the home and community environment. A final sentence of the book refers to "pervasive leadership, indigenous innovation, and team learning" as necessary elements to transform school cultures into high-performance learning environments (209).

Question Two

How can belief in the ability and promise of the children be cultivated?

This question prompts a consideration of other questions related to race/ethnicity and gender. We have reviewed the historical origins of the racial prejudices and deficit thinking that contribute to the achievement gap, and contend that powerful leadership in high-poverty schools begins at the level of beliefs and attitudes. Cultivating belief in the ability and promise of the children does not seem to be an issue for the principals of color in the research we reviewed or in our own case studies. However, not all the principals in successful high-poverty schools are persons of color, nor are they women. We do not believe that being an effective leader in a high-poverty school requires being African American, Hispanic, or even female. It does require authenticity and respect for people from all cultures and backgrounds. Only a principal who values the children and believes they can learn and achieve at high levels will be able to make a difference in beliefs and attitudes of faculty and staff.

From our perspective, leadership that alters the perceived destinies of children from low-income families begins with the self-examination of beliefs and attitudes. Reflective practice is essential to learning. Reflective practice as first defined by Dewey includes "active, persistent, and careful consideration of any belief or supposed form of knowledge in the light of the grounds that support it and the further conclusions to which it tends . . ." (1938, 9). It requires the individual to reconstruct events, emotions, beliefs, and attitudes through reflecting on his or her experiences and interpretations of them. "Meaningful learning occurs only through self-examination of assumptions, patterns of interactions, and the operating premises of action. Critical self-reflection therefore, represents the essence of transformational learning" (Villani and Ward 2001, 48). The processes of self-inquiry and reflective learning in conversation and dialogue are summarized by Tremmel as "a dance-like pattern, simultaneously involved in design and in playing various roles in virtual and real worlds while, at the same time, remaining detached enough to observe and feel the action that is occurring and to respond" (1993, 436). This pattern will lead to discomfort as one confronts espoused attitudes and beliefs against the true realities. Prejudices and biases will emerge. Research findings consistently cite teacher biases as a factor in the low achievement of children in high-poverty schools. Such findings confirm the critical importance of cultivating belief in the ability and promise of the children. Successfully facilitating a group process of reflective learning is contingent upon the vision of the leader, a willingness to shift paradigms, to face one's misconceptions, and to move toward new learning that will lead to quality educational experiences for all students. Only after traveling their own paths of self-discovery can leaders engage faculty and staff members in journeys of self-reflection.

Transformative leaders start with where people are, creating safe spaces for the honest examination of assumptions and beliefs. An exchange of perspectives in a conversation can start the process of perspective transformation that accompanies reflection on experience (Mezirow 1991). Resources for such processes include Wheatley's (2002) conversation starter questions, such as: What is my faith in the future? What do I believe about others? What am I willing to notice in my world? and What is my unique contribution to the whole? Another resource for leading a school's faculty and staff through a process of reflective learning is detailed by Senge (1990). A learning resource for leaders and groups is the *Fifth Discipline Fieldbook* (Senge, Kleiner, Roberts, Ross, and Smith 1994) with field-tested individual and group exercises on developing personal mastery, surfacing mental models, developing shared vision, and team learning. As explored in chapter 6, reading Heifetz (1994), Goodman (2001), and Wheatley (2002) will deepen understanding of how leadership can bring about adaptive change in beliefs, values, and behaviors. The ultimate goal of any reflective learning process would be for the entire faculty and staff to abandon deficit thinking about children and families living in poverty. Given the persisting stereotypes and prejudices about poverty and racial/ethnic difference, achieving this goal will take time.

Question Three

How can professional development contribute to successful high-poverty schools?

Ongoing professional development is one avenue through which principals can provide experiences designed to cultivate belief in the ability and promise of the children as well as give teachers the opportunity to explore together what is known about effective instruction for poor and minority children. In the four case studies we reviewed in chapter 5, providing professional development to support the work of the teachers was one of the three best leadership practices identified through our comparative analysis. A particularly interesting study completed in Louisiana (Hair, Kraft, and Allen 2001) demonstrates the power of professional development to support and enhance student achievement in high-poverty schools. Supported by a grant, the Louisiana Staff Development Council undertook research to investigate the role that staff development plays "in assisting schools with high percentages of children in poverty to attain exemplary academic achievement" (3). They chose as sites for the study twelve schools rated as academically above average for at least two years in a row where 80 to 100 percent of the students qualified for free or reduced lunch. On-site visits were made to the schools, and interviews and focus groups conducted. The following five factors existed in the professional development programs of all the high-performing, high-poverty schools in the study:

1. Staff development was definitely results driven.
2. Many forms of job-embedded staff development were evident.
3. Staff development emphasized a balance between content (what teachers teach) and pedagogy (how teachers teach).
4. Faculty collaboration was viewed as critical to improved practice.
5. An instructional leader guided the learning process for teachers and provided the resources needed. (9)

The researchers also identified eight common success factors. One factor reinforces the importance of high expectations: "The principal and entire staff have a strong sense of efficacy—they believe in the power of teaching and their own ability to ensure that every student learns, regardless of the obstacles. In fact the teachers could be described as 'human bulldozers,' ready to 'level' any mountain put before them!" (7) The same could be said of the faculty and staff at Harrison and Newfield.

Many resources and professional development programs are available to help principals with the task of educating beliefs and attitudes of faculty and staff about children and families living in poverty. For example, Ruby Payne (1998) provides workshops designed to acquaint educators with what she calls a framework for understanding poverty. Payne's approach comes from the culture of poverty paradigm, but principals including Aurthur Perkins report that her materials have helped faculty and staff understand and interact more productively with children from low-income families. The Efficacy Institute (www.efficacy.org), located in Boston, also offers resources and professional development programs that can lead to more productive attitudes about intelligence, teaching, and the role of effort in learning. Founded by Jeff Howard, the premise of the Efficacy Institute's work with schools across the country is that intelligence is a developmental process, not something that is fixed at birth or by socioeconomic or cultural factors. His group teaches teachers how to give children tools to reach high levels of academic achievement. Lindsey, Robins, and Terrell (1999) have written an informational manual for school leaders to use in designing educational experiences to promote "cultural proficiency" among faculty and staff. They write, "Cultural *proficiency* represents either the policies, practices, and procedures of a school or the values and behaviors of an individual that enable that school or person to interact effectively in a culturally diverse environment" (30). Many of the exercises are framed as self-reflections.

Educational leaders need to undertake the complex task of developing programs and workshops where the issues of poverty and educating children who live in poverty can be addressed. Effective professional development is systemic and comprised not of one-time workshops but of ongoing attention in a variety of formats throughout the academic year. Such sustained effort requires a principal convinced that beliefs and attitudes about poor and minority children are limiting learning and achievement. Faculty and staff can be involved in designing professional development experiences that give them the opportunity to carefully examine their attitudes and beliefs about poverty and educating children who live in poverty. Professional development can include activities that allow educators to immerse themselves in the lives of the children in order to understand their needs. During such a comprehensive process, educators will continue to reframe their beliefs and attitudes. Only through systemic, sustained, professional development will educators come to understand the complex issues of poverty in our schools and society from political, economic, cultural, and educational perspectives.

Question Four

How can collective leadership be developed in a school?

This is a question that may require serious reflection from those inclined toward one-dimensional, *take-charge* leadership. Effective leadership in high-poverty schools requires "new cultures that are simultaneously supportive and pushy" (Fullan 2003, 62). The point is that addressing the challenges of learning and achievement in a high-poverty school requires a supportive community with collective leadership coming from all corners. Perkins was lauded for having created a subculture of teacher leaders. Both Perkins and Perez-Dickson have deliberately cultivated within their schools a sense of family. Working toward the education of all children is enhanced by a strong sense of family, where each individual's perspective is valued and respected. Some may be more comfortable with the family metaphor; others with creating a team. It doesn't matter what you call it—family or team, the metaphor does not matter.

Emerging definitions of effective leadership emphasize that leading requires a collective effort. Drath and Palus (1994), for example, define leadership as *meaning-making* or *sense-making*. "Whenever people are doing something together for any period of time extended enough to form a community, we can usefully think of the striving to make things make sense, to create meaning out of that experience, as the process of leadership—however that process plays out and with whatever participation by various individuals" (25). Lambert (1998) also describes leadership as embedded in the school community and implying shared responsibility. She writes:

> The key notion in this definition is that leadership is about learning together, and constructing meaning and knowledge collectively and collaboratively. It involves opportunities to surface and mediate perceptions, values, beliefs, information, and assumptions through continuing conversations; to inquire about and generate ideas together; to seek to reflect upon and make sense of work in the light of shared beliefs and new information; and to create actions that grow out of these new understandings. (5–6)

Fullan explains, "It is the combined forces of shared leadership that makes a difference. School leadership is a collective enterprise" (2003, xv). We agree with Fullan's perspective that leaders who combine moral purpose with relational trust will make a difference. Teachers at Harrison and Newfield feel like part of a family or a team, a reflection of the relational trust established by Perkins and Perez-Dickson. The schools exemplify meaningful collaboration as faculty members work together to diagnose problems and create better learning experiences for the children. Principals, faculty, and staff assume collective responsibility for leadership.

Question Five

How are meaningful partnerships created with families and the community?

Bolman and Deal write, "Effective leadership is a relationship rooted in community" (1995, 56). The community of a school is multilevel and a principal must have the ability to build relationships on all levels. Perkins and Perez-Dickson are personally involved with the issues and lives of their students. Both regularly intervene to make the life situations of students better. Students seek them out for hugs and thrive with their attention. Each has supported and cultivated relationships of trust with families, and reached out to the larger community to find resources for the school and individual families. Each values parent involvement and treats parents as important partners in the educational process.

Henderson and Mapp (2002) researched the impact of parent involvement on student achievement. They focused on a wide range of schools, from early childhood to high school, from all over the country with diverse populations and socioeconomic needs. They found improved student achievement in schools where school leaders established positive and genuine relationships with the parents. When the relationships were regarded as genuine, this effect held across all economic, racial/ethnic, and educational backgrounds for students at all ages. Based on this research, Henderson and Mapp urge leaders to create programs that engage the parents in supporting their child's learning at home. The more families support their children, the better they do in school. Perkins and Perez-Dickson have parent programs to assist in parenting skills and understanding homework assignments. A strong element fostering parental involvement is that each parent is treated with respect and dignity.

Quint (1994) describes how B. F. Day Elementary in Seattle became a community school through reaching out to the community for help in meeting the needs of large numbers of homeless students and their families. Epstein (1995) is a primary spokesperson for the school/family/community partnership movement. Defining caring as the core concept for building a partnership, she writes, "Research results . . . indicate that caring communities can be built, on purpose; that they include families that might not become involved on their own; and that, by their own reports, just about all families, students, and teachers believe that partnerships are important for helping students succeed across the grades" (703–4). Community partnerships also thrive with collaborative leadership. "A principal's willingness and ability to engage in collaboration are essential to the success of the initiative" (Decker and Decker 2000, 53). Collaborative relationships involve components such as credibility, shared concerns, trust building, shared decision making and celebration. Community partnerships exist on a continuum. Some are formal, like Harrison School's Adopt-a-School partnerships with six different community groups and agencies. Some involve simple one-time, one-on-one projects. Still others develop into full-blown partnerships complete with shared governance.

A relatively new development is the concept of a full-service school, a concept particularly helpful in high-poverty areas. "Full-service schools are based on the premise that no single agency or organization can substantially improve the lives of children and families, especially at-risk children and families" (Decker and Decker 2000, 66). Some of these schools become full-service community centers open year-round that house programs such as health and dental clinics, individual and family counseling, mentoring, extended-day programs, family welfare service, adult education, and others. The programs are typically available to everyone in the community. According to researchers Dryfoos and Maguire, "Community schools work to create a more effective school environment, encouraging small classes with well-trained teachers and high standards. With partners from community agencies to address behavioral and social issues, teachers can concentrate on teaching" (2002, 13). A goal of a full-service school is to provide additional support to children with significant barriers to learning.

A supporter of the community school concept as a way to build social capital for children in need through community initiatives, Maeroff (1998) describes successful programs that confront factors that obstruct academic achievement. The programs have in common the cultivation of four main objectives: "a sense of connectedness, a sense of well-being, a sense of academic initiative, and a sense of knowing" (6–7). He believes that the problems of the children are community problems that must be confronted through action at the level of community. Yet, Maeroff writes, "The relevant social indicators affecting children who live in poverty have been cited so many times that the public has grown inured to them" (11). In spite of complacency, those who are creating full-service community schools, he believes, are getting schools involved with issues such as "housing, health, the environment, employment, and civil rights, for instance" (15). Because problems in schools reflect and are intertwined with problems in the larger community, "the implication for contemporary schools is that they must regard themselves as part of a larger landscape and, like trees radiating roots, extend linkages in many directions at once" (15).

Summary

Principals who wrestle with and revisit the five questions we have raised will undoubtedly find new questions as they confront the need for change in schools and society. We have presented opinions and information as a basis for thinking about the questions. In no way are we suggesting definitive answers. The questions imply layers of understanding and a logical progression for action. Although not the only important questions, reflecting on them will lead a principal to continually assess what is known and unknown about successful high-poverty schools, to understand the critical importance of beliefs and attitudes, to arrange for ongoing focused professional development, to foster collective leadership, and to engage in meaningful partnerships with families and the community.

THE NEED FOR CHANGE

According to Chamberlin (2001), "poverty is perpetuated by stereotypes which misrepresent reality, by the historic dependence of our society on the employed poor built into inherited institutional structures, by the failure of those in power to recognize the true dimensions of poverty's long-term blight, by the many ways in which the poverty sector benefits the non-poor" (70). The need for change in society and schools cannot be overemphasized. The needs of poor children cry out for changes in how we do things as a country and as educators. Nationally, a long-standing and documented achievement gap continues to grow between students from low-income and middle/upper-class families and between racial/ethnic/language minority students and white English-speaking students. Human costs of child poverty are enormous and extend beyond the realms of education. Apple (1996) writes, "Many people are able to distance themselves from these realities. There is almost a pathological distancing among the affluent. Yet, how can one not be morally outraged at the growing gap between rich and poor, the persistence of hunger and homelessness, the deadly absence of medical care, the degradations of poverty?" (41).

Poverty's continuing existence in their lives does lasting harm to children. According to Sherman (1994), damaging outcomes can result from lack of food, housing problems, family stress, neighborhood problems, and fewer resources for learning. Growing up in poverty can adversely affect a child's health, and physical, social, and emotional development. Millions of American children who live in poverty during their formative years face a risk of impaired development. Researchers have gathered new evidence about the importance of the first years of a child's life and the impact of poverty on children's development. For example, "poor children are 2 to 3 times more likely to have stunted growth (unusually low height for the child's age)" (Sherman 1994, 15). Poor children are more likely to suffer from asthma, iron deficiency, diarrhea, pneumonia, repeated tonsillitis, and dental problems.

Recent research in brain development has demonstrated that the brain is particularly sensitive during the early years of a child's life and that poverty poses a serious threat to a child's brain development. Brain development is very sensitive to environmental stimulation, particularly from the prenatal period through the first years of a child's life. Children who live in poverty are more exposed to risk factors that can adversely influence brain development. These risk factors include inadequate nutrition, substance abuse, maternal depression, environmental toxins, trauma/abuse, and the quality of daily care. A family situation of severe poverty can lead to inadequate nutrition. Children deprived of proper nutrition during this critical time of brain development score much lower on standardized tests of reading comprehension, vocabulary, mathematics, and general knowledge. Malnutrition also leads to delayed motor skills, delayed physical growth, and social withdrawal. Challenging physical conditions can be compounded by psychological difficulties such as poor self-esteem and isolation. "Research on the impact of poverty on children suggests that avoiding the adverse consequences of deep poverty in early childhood is key for the healthy cognitive development of children" (Duncan and Brooks-Gunn 2001, 65).

The effects of their environment on children who live in poverty have not been accurately measured (Lewitt, Terman, and Behrman 1997). Environment is social as well as physical. Children who live in poverty may experience traumas in their first years of life that result in depression, extreme anxiety, poor attachments to others, and antisocial behaviors. These traumas are often inflicted unintentionally as stressed parents struggle to make ends meet. Crowded living conditions, hopelessness, substance abuse, and other factors can lead to parental neglect and abuse of their children. Children who suffer such traumas can develop a higher propensity for violence later on in life. Adolescents who live in poverty have a higher incidence of teenage pregnancy and experience more violent crimes. For example, "Low-income adolescents might be expected to fight as a reaction to rejection or because of frustration about their inferior status" (Brantlinger 1993, 57). In her research into perceptions of affluent and impoverished youth about social class, Brantlinger found that "the narratives of all adolescents revealed a mind-set that linked poverty with lack of school success; both [poverty and lack of school success] were the outcome of (negative) personal qualities. This tendency to personalize blame for situations resulted in both feelings of unworthiness and a basic tolerance for stratifying conditions" (42).

Healthy self-esteem can be a casualty of growing up in poverty. A child who grows up with low self-esteem suffers from a serious blight. Societal stereotypes about the inferiority of the poor can become internalized stigmas. For example, adolescents from poor and minority families described how they perceived teachers and administrators to feel about them: "They think the kids are no good, I guess that's it. . . . The truth is, that is how many people (other students) feel. I don't even give a shit what he (the teacher) thinks, so it doesn't matter to me because I know he don't care if I live or die. If they don't care about you, why the hell should you do what they want you to do?" (Wexler 1992, 38–39). Self-esteem refers to the evaluative views and feelings about the self that express degrees of personal satisfaction or dissatisfaction. It is the person's implicit and explicit comparison of his or her self-concept in an area (such as academics) to standards for the self in that area that determines whether self-esteem is high or low (Bandura 1986). It is important to distinguish theoretically between self-concept and self-esteem. Self-concept is regarded as primarily the descriptive aspects of self-perception that are not evaluative in terms of expressing satisfaction or dissatisfaction with the attributes that are involved. Factors that can outweigh the negative effects of poverty and lead children from low socioeconomic situations toward being academically successful are a positive self-concept, strong self-esteem and personal values, and aspirations (Werner 1995).

Although various factors can compromise the academic achievement of children who live in poverty, no factor is more damaging to children's achievement than low expectations stemming from the belief that poverty equals low academic ability. Low achievement of students from low-income families can no longer be accepted as their destiny. As educators, we can no longer blame the victims for the achievement gap. Both Perkins and Perez-Dickson were respected for having high expectations for the children, faculty, staff, and parents. Teachers at Harrison and Newfield were expected to teach students well. As Perez-Dickson states, "Socioeconomic status does not determine ability. I do not believe that and that thinking is not fostered here." Examination of standardized test results from both schools clearly indicates that setting high expectations works. Setting high expectations means challenging students. If students are not challenged, they become comfortable in learning environments where the lowest expectations are the norm. Challenging learning environments are motivational. They encourage children to take risks and to constructively learn from their mistakes. Educators who encourage measured academic risk help all students to reach higher learning levels (Jones 2003).

As reflected in this brief overview of some of the major effects of poverty on development, school personnel in high-poverty areas must reckon with the ravages of poverty in attending to children's academic, personal, and social needs. By the time children growing up in low-income families get to school, many of the effects of life in poverty are clearly visible. As educators we must address the needs of children living in poverty at a variety of levels, including physical and emotional health, before we can begin to meet their learning needs. We must also work with their family members, providing emotional support and connecting them with resources if at all possible. Addressing the complexities of poverty and building school learning environments where children who live in poverty can achieve at high levels may seem daunting. The schools of Aurthur Perkins and Carmen Perez-Dickson are models of how schools must be if the needs of children are to be met.

CHALLENGES OF LEADERSHIP FOR SOCIAL JUSTICE

The fundamental challenge of leadership for social justice in high-poverty schools is the economic injustice of the larger society. As a society, we need to address why we are willing to have a child poverty rate that is two to three times higher than other Western industrialized nations. Biddle (2001) explains as well as anyone that the continuing existence of child poverty is not a necessary reality, that childhood poverty can be reduced.

If poor children suffer real disadvantages in life that depress their chances in education, the obvious way to help them out is to reduce the rate of childhood poverty, and it does not take a rocket scientist to figure out how to do this. Other industrialized countries have long since instituted social programs that reduce poverty for children—such as universal healthcare systems, tax-supported daycare programs, child allowances, extra support for single parents, crisis-intervention programs, and the like. (15)

Childhood poverty can be reduced, but as a society we apparently are misinformed or lack the will. As Chamberlin eloquently explains, "Both leaders and the public at large need to understand that poverty is perpetuated by stereotypes which misrepresent reality . . . by the failure of those in power to understand the true nature of its dimensions" (2001, 156). Educators are among those without full comprehension of the complexity and blight that is poverty. Because colleges do not provide coursework on the issues of poverty, too many future teachers and administrators leave preparation programs with common societal attitudes and deficit-thinking stereotypes intact: they blame the poor for being poor, and they see children of the poor with eyes of pity. They look only on the surface and remain caught between the claims of justice and privilege.

As with poverty, we have the knowledge to reduce the achievement gap, but do we have the will? Larson and Murtadha write, "To social justice theorists, lofty visions of equality and opportunity are important, but not sufficient for bringing greater educational equity into being. . . . Throughout history, creating greater social justice in society and its institutions has required the commitment of dedicated leaders" (2002, 135). They also assert this note of realism: "School leaders who believe that their schools are equitable for all children regularly enact programs and policies that they assume are fair and serve the academic and social interests of all students. But many are misguided, in part, because they are not sufficiently aware of the differences that limit children's and their families' freedoms to achieve" (156). We agree and further contend that layers of prejudice and decades of deficit thinking block the collective will of society. For too long, too many educators have accepted the achievement gap as destiny for children from low-income families—but calls for social justice in schools are becoming louder.

According to Larson and Murtadha, "Researchers in educational administration who believe that injustice in our schools and communities is

neither natural nor inevitable loosely coalesce under an umbrella of inquiry called leadership for social justice" (2002, 135). Leadership for social justice in schools is challenging because the issues are vast and interrelated with social justice issues of race, class, and gender in the larger
society. These interrelationships are reflected in the fact that teacher bias
and lack of financial resources recur as themes in explanations for the
achievement gap. Changing teachers' belief systems and garnering fiscal
and material resources are equally challenging social justice leadership issues. An additional challenge is that "because poor and minority populations have learned to mistrust public leaders, well-intentioned school leaders often have difficulty earning their confidence and cooperation"
(Larson and Murtadha 2002, 147).

Dissatisfaction with the status quo, however, seems to be leading many
persons from all levels of education in passionate new directions. Fullan
(2003) defines leadership's moral imperative to include improving the learning of all students and closing the achievement gap. Shields (2003) reminds
us that good intentions are not enough, and that the role of the transformative leader in multicultural communities of difference is to "use the criteria
of justice, democracy, empathy, and optimism to assess and guide their
school communities" (247). Furman claims "that educational leadership as a
field is focusing more and more on what leadership is *for*; that it is the *moral
purposes* of educational leadership that are emerging as the central focus"
(2003, 1). She elaborates, "Leadership for social justice suggests the moral
purpose of creating schools that serve *all* children well, not just mainstream
children, but children who have been marginalized or poorly served in the
past" (1). Furman also argues for schools to become more democratic as
communities. Although we cannot eliminate the systemic economic injustice
that perpetuates poverty, we can become informed about its complex realities. As citizens, we can advocate for social rights such as those elaborated
in Article 25 of the Universal Declaration of Human Rights, passed by the
General Assembly of the United Nations on December 10, 1948:

1. Everyone has the right to a standard of living adequate for the health
   and well-being of himself and his family, including food, clothing,
   housing and medical care and necessary social services, and the right to
   security in the event of unemployment, sickness, disability, widowhood,
   old age or other lack of livelihood in circumstances beyond his control.

2. Motherhood and childhood are entitled to special care and assistance. All children, whether born in or out of wedlock, shall enjoy the same social protection. (Roosevelt 2002, 209)

We can make changes in our schools that provide children with the protection of a coalescence of significant adults (Quint 1994). We can welcome parents with respect as equal partners in the education of their children. We can change school policies and practices that create inequity of opportunity. We can support professional development that gives teachers the attitudes, knowledge, and skills to teach all children well. And finally, to make a difference for children in high-poverty schools, we can continue to explore the questions we have posed in this chapter.

REFLECTION

We have sought in this book to confront the prejudices and deficit thinking that rationalize the achievement gap, to present information to educators who may be ignorant of poverty's complexities, and to argue through the case study examples of Aurthur Perkins and Carmen Perez-Dickson that leaders make a difference for children in high-poverty schools. We hope the educational leaders who will end discriminatory policies and teaching practices that limit children's futures are reading this book. The leaders we describe offer hope to all with the courage to accept the challenge of creating caring and academically successful high-poverty schools. Dedicated leaders who make a difference in the life chances of students in high-poverty schools make a difference ultimately to the larger society. Our elected officials may choose not to eliminate systemic economic injustice in our lifetimes, but as educators we can become lifelines to children and families living in poverty. In the end, maybe that will make all the difference. In the words of hooks (2000):

Solidarity with the poor is the only path that can lead our nation back to a vision of community that can effectively challenge and eliminate violence and exploitation. It invites us to embrace an ethic of compassion and sharing that will renew a spirit of loving kindness and communion that can sustain and enable us to live in harmony with the whole world. (49)

References

Ah Nee-Benham, M. K. P., and J. E. Cooper. 1998. *Let my spirit soar! Narratives of diverse women in school leadership*. Thousand Oaks, Calif.: Corwin Press.

Apple, M. W. 1996. *Cultural politics and education*. New York: Teachers College Press.

Bandura, A. 1986. *Social foundations of thought and action: A social cognitive theory*. Upper Saddle River, N.J.: Prentice Hall.

Barth, P., K. Haycock, H. Jackson, K. Mora, P. Ruiz, S. Robinson, and A. Wilkins. 1999. *Dispelling the myth: High poverty schools exceeding expectations*. Washington, D.C.: Education Trust.

Barth, R. S. 1990. *Improving schools from within: Teachers, parents, and principals can make a difference*. San Francisco, Calif.: Jossey-Bass.

Bell, L. I. 2002–2003. Strategies that close the gap. *Educational Leadership* 60, no. 4:32–34.

Biddle, B. J., ed. 2001. *Social class, poverty, and education: Policy and practice*. New York: Routledge Falmer.

Bolman, L. G., and T. E. Deal. 1995. *Leading with soul: An uncommon journey of spirit*. San Francisco, Calif.: Jossey-Bass.

Boushey, H., C. Brocht, B. Gunderson, and J. Bernstein. 2001. Hardships in America: The real story of working families. *Economic Policy Institute,* EPI Report.

Brantlinger, E. A. 1993. *The politics of social class in secondary school: Views of affluent and impoverished youth*. New York: Teachers College Press.

Brown, D. R. 1999. Harrison students score big on exam. *Peoria Journal Star*, November 3.

Brown, L., and E. Pollitt. 1996. Malnutrition, poverty and intellectual development, *Scientific American* 274, no. 2:38–43.

Bryk, A. S., and B. Schneider. 2002. *Trust in schools: A core resource for improvement*. New York: Russell Sage Foundation.

Carlson, K. G., S. Shagle-Shah, and M. D. Ramirez. 1999. *Leave no child behind: An examination of Chicago's most improved schools and the leadership strategies behind them.* Chicago: Chicago Schools Academic Accountability Council, October.

Carter, M., and L. T. Fenwick. 2001. Keeping a close watch: A cultural philosophy of school change. *NASSP Bulletin* 85, no. 624:15–22.

Carter, S. C. 2002a. *No excuses: Seven principals of low-income schools who set the standards for high achievement.* Washington, D.C.: Heritage Foundation.

———. 2002b. *No excuses: Lessons from high-performing, high-poverty schools.* Washington, D.C.: Heritage Foundation.

Catania, P. 2001. The urban principalship: Making a difference. *Principal* 81 (September): 14–16.

Chamberlin, J. G. 2001. *Upon whom we depend: The American poverty system.* New York: Peter Lang.

Children's Defense Fund. 2002. Number of poor children in America rises for the first time in eight years. September 24, 2002. At www.childrensdefense.org/release020924.php (accessed July 7, 2003).

———. 2003. Child poverty. At www.childrensdefense.org/fs_chpov.php (accessed July 7, 2003).

Connell, R. W. 1994. Poverty and education. *Harvard Educational Review* 64, no. 2. At www.edreview.org/issues/harvard94/1994/su94/s94conn.htm (accessed July 2000, authorization required).

Cottle, T. J. 2001. *At peril: Stories of injustice.* Amherst: University of Massachusetts Press.

Dauber, S., and J. Epstein. 1993. Parents' attitudes and practice of involvement in inner-city elementary and middle schools. In *Families and schools in a pluralistic society*, edited by N. Chavkin, 53–71. Albany: State University of New York Press.

Decker, L. E., and V. A. Decker. 2000. *Engaging families and communities: Pathways to educational success.* Fairfax, Va.: National Community Education Association.

Delpit, L. 1995. *Other people's children: Cultural conflict in the classroom.* New York: New Press.

Dewey, J. 1938. *Experience and education.* New York: Macmillan.

Dillard, C. 1995. Leading with her life: An African American feminist reinterpretation of leadership for an urban high school principal. *Educational Administration Quarterly* 31, no. 4:539–63.

Drath, W. H., and C. J. Palus. 1994. *Making common sense: Leadership as meaning-making in a community of practice.* Greensboro, N.C.: Center for Creative Leadership.

Drazen, S. 1992. *Student achievement and family community poverty: Twenty years of education reform.* A paper presented at the annual meeting of the Eastern Psychological Association, April, at Boston, Massachusetts.

Dryfoos, J., and S. Maguire. 2002. *Inside full-service community schools.* Thousand Oaks, Calif.: Corwin Press.

Duncan, G. J., and J. Brooks-Gunn. 2001. Poverty, welfare reform, and children's achievement. In *Social class, poverty, and education: Policy and practice,* edited by B. J. Biddle, 49–75. New York: Routledge Falmer.

Edmonds, R. R. 1979. Some schools work and more can. *Social Policy* 9, no. 5:28–32.

——. 1986. Characteristics of effective schools. In *The school achievement of minority children: New perspectives,* edited by U. Neisser, 93–104. Hillsdale, N.J.: Lawrence Erlbaum.

Ehrenreich, B. 2001a. *Nickel and dimed: On not getting by in America.* New York: Henry Holt and Company.

——. 2001b. America's torrent of need. *Los Angeles Times,* August 5.

Epstein, J. L. 1995. School/family/community partnerships. *Phi Delta Kappan* 76, no. 9:701–12.

Foley, D. E. 1997. Deficit thinking models based on culture: The anthropological protest. In *The evolution of deficit thinking: Educational thought and practice,* edited by R. R. Valencia, 113–31. Washington, D.C.: Falmer Press.

Frank, V. F. 2003. Closing the divide. *National Staff Development Council Results* (March): 1, 6.

Fullan, M. 1993. *Change forces: Probing the depths of educational reform.* Bristol, Penn.: Falmer Press.

——. 1997. *What's worth fighting for in the principalship.* New York: Teachers College Press.

——. 1999. *Change forces: The sequel.* Philadelphia, Penn.: Falmer Press.

——. 2003. *The moral imperative of school leadership.* Thousand Oaks, Calif.: Corwin Press.

Furman, G. 2003. The 2002 UCEA presidential address. *UCEA Review* 45, no. 1:1–5.

Gay, G. 2000. *Culturally responsive teaching: Theory, research, and practice.* New York: Teachers College Press.

Goodman, D. J. 2001. *Promoting diversity and social justice: Educating people from privileged groups.* Thousand Oaks, Calif.: Sage Publications.

Haberman, M. 1995. *Star teachers of children in poverty.* Indianapolis, Ind.: Kappa Delta Pi.

——. 1999. *Star principals: Serving children in poverty.* Indianapolis, Ind.: Kappa Delta Pi.

Hafer, A. 2000. *Prisoners of the paradigm*. Boulder, Colo.: FalCo Books.

Hair, D., B. Kraft, and A. Allen. 2001. *Louisiana staff development council's end of grant report*. National Staff Development Council Project ADVANCE Mini-Grant. At www.nsdc.org/library/results/res2-03rich.html (accessed February 17, 2003).

Haycock, K. 2001. Closing the achievement gap. *Educational Leadership* 58, no. 6:6–11.

———. 2002–2003. Toward a fair distribution of teacher talent. *Educational Leadership* 60, no. 4:11–15.

Heifetz, R. A. 1994. *Leadership without easy answers*. Cambridge, Mass.: Harvard University Press.

Henderson, A. T., and K. L. Mapp. 2002. *A new wave of evidence: The impact of school, family and community connections on student achievement*. At www.sedl.org/connections/resources/evidence.pdf (accessed July 7, 2003).

hooks, b. 2000. *Where we stand: Class matters*. New York: Routledge.

Jackson, D. B. 2003. Education reform as if student agency mattered: Academic microcultures and student identity. *Phi Delta Kappan* 84, no. 8:579–85.

Johnson, J. F., and R. Asera, eds. 1999. *Hope for urban education*. Austin: Charles A. Dana Center at the University of Texas.

Jones, S. J. 2003. *Blueprint for student success: A guide to research-based teaching practices K–12*. Thousand Oaks, Calif.: Corwin Press.

Kozol, J. 1995. *Amazing grace: The lives of children and the conscience of a nation*. New York: Crown Publishers.

Ladson-Billings, G. 1994. *The dreamkeepers: Successful teachers of African American children*. San Francisco: Jossey-Bass.

———. 2001. *Crossing over to Canaan: The journeys of new teachers in diverse classrooms*. San Francisco: Jossey-Bass.

Lambert, L. 1998. *Building leadership capacity in schools*. Alexandria, Va.: Association for Supervision and Curriculum Development.

Larson, C. L., and K. Murtadha. 2002. Leadership for social justice. In *The educational leadership challenge: Redefining leadership for the 21st century*, edited by J. Murphy, 134–61. Chicago: National Society for the Study of Education.

Lewitt, E., D. Terman, and R. Behrman. 1997. Children and poverty, analysis, and recommendations. *The future of children* 7, no. 2:8–9.

Lindsey, R. B., K. N. Robins, and R. D. Terrell. 1999. *Cultural proficiency: A manual for school leaders*. Thousand Oaks, Calif.: Corwin Press.

Lomotey, K. 1989. *African-American principals: School leadership and success*. New York: Greenwood Press.

———. 1993. African-American principals: Bureaucrat/administrators and ethno-humanists. *Urban Education* 27, no. 4:395–412.

Lu, H. 2003. Low-income children in the United States: A brief demographic pro-file. National Center for Children in Poverty at nccp.org/media/cpf03-text.pdf (accessed July 7, 2003).

Lyman, L. L. 2000. *How do they know you care? The principal's challenge*. New York: Teachers College Press.

———. 2003. Soul sisters: Origins and accomplishments of a unique partnership. *Journal of Women in Educational Leadership* 1, no. 1:43–60.

Lyman, L. L., and C. J. Villani. 2002. The complexity of poverty: A missing com-ponent of educational leadership programs. *Journal of School Leadership* 12, no. 3:246–80.

Maeroff, G. I. 1998. *Altered destinies: Making life better for schoolchildren in need*. New York: St. Martin's Griffin.

Marshall, K. 1996. No one ever said it would be easy. *Phi Delta Kappan* 78, no. 4:307–8.

McLeod, W. T., ed. 1987. *Collins dictionary and thesaurus*. London: Collins.

Menchaca, M. 1997. Early racist discourses: Roots of deficit thinking. In *The evolution of deficit thinking: Educational thought and practice*, edited by R. R. Valencia, 13–40. Washington, D.C.: Falmer Press.

Mezirow, J. 1991. *Transformative dimensions of adult learning*. San Francisco, Calif.: Jossey-Bass.

Miller, L. S. 1995. *An American imperative: Accelerating minority educational advancement*. New Haven, Conn.: Yale University Press.

Morris, J. E. 2002. A "communally bonded" school for African American fami-lies, and a community. *Phi Delta Kappan* 84, no. 3:230–34.

Mortimore, P., P. Sammons, L. Stoll, D. Lewis, and R. Ecob. 1988. *School mat-ters: The junior years*. London: Open Books.

Murrell, P. C. 2002. *African-centered pedagogy: Developing schools of achieve-ment for African American children*. Albany: State University of New York Press.

Murtadha-Watts, K. 1999. Spirited sisters: Spirituality and the activism of African American women in educational leadership. In *School leadership: Expanding horizons of the mind and spirit*, edited by L. Fenwick. Proceedings of the Na-tional Council for Professors of Educational Administration. Lancaster, Penn.: Technomic.

Nadel, W., and S. Sagawa. 2002. *America's forgotten children: Child poverty in rural America*. Save the Children Federation at www.savethechildren.org (ac-cessed July 7, 2003).

National Center on Addiction and Substance Abuse. 2001. *2001 CASA national survey of American attitudes on substance abuse VI: Teens*. New York: NCASA at Columbia University.

Nieto, S. M. 2002–2003. Profoundly multicultural questions. *Educational Leadership* 60, no. 4:7–10.

Noddings, N. 1984. *Caring: A feminine approach to ethics and moral education.* Berkeley: University of California Press.

Orfield, G., E. D. Frankenberg, and C. Lee. 2002–2003. The resurgence of school segregation. *Educational Leadership* 60, no. 4:16–20.

Payne, R. K. 1998. *A framework for understanding poverty.* Baytown, Tex.: AhaProcess.

Pearl, A. 1997a. Cultural and accumulated environmental deficit models. In *The evolution of deficit thinking: Educational thought and practice*, edited by R. R. Valencia, 132–59. Washington, D.C.: Falmer Press.

———. 1997b. Democratic education as an alternative to deficit thinking. In *The evolution of deficit thinking: Educational thought and practice*, edited by R. R. Valencia, 211–41. Washington, D.C.: Falmer Press.

Polakow, V. 1993. *Lives on the edge: Mothers and their children in the other America.* Chicago: University of Chicago Press.

Quint, S. 1994. *Schooling homeless children.* New York: Teachers College Press.

Reyes, P., J. D. Scribner, and A. P. Scribner, eds. 1999. *Lessons from high-performing Hispanic schools.* New York: Teachers College Press.

Riester, A. F., V. Pursch, and L. Skrla. 2002. Principals for social justice: Leaders of school success for children from low-income homes. *Journal of School Leadership* 12, no. 3:281–304.

Rooney, J. 2003. Principals who care: A personal reflection. *Educational Leadership* 60, no. 6:76–78.

Roosevelt, D. B. 2002. *Grandmere.* New York: Warner Books.

Ryan, W. 1971. *Blaming the victim.* New York: Vintage Books.

Scherer, M. 2002–2003. The line and the gap. *Educational Leadership* 60, no. 4:5.

Scheurich, J. J. 1998. Highly successful and loving, public elementary schools populated mainly by low SES children of color: Core beliefs and cultural characteristics. *Urban Education* 33, no. 4:451–92.

Schorr, L. 1988. *Within our reach: Breaking the cycle of disadvantage.* New York: Doubleday.

Scribner, A. P. 1999. High-performing Hispanic schools: An introduction. In *Lessons from high-performing Hispanic schools*, edited by P. Reyes, J. D. Scribner, and A. P. Scribner, 1–18. New York: Teachers College Press.

Scribner, J. D., and P. Reyes. 1999. Creating learning communities for high-performing Hispanic students: A conceptual framework. In *Lessons from high-performing Hispanic schools*, edited by P. Reyes, J. D. Scribner, and A. P. Scribner, 188–210. New York: Teachers College Press.

Scribner, J. D., M. D. Young, and A. Pedroza. 1999. Building collaborative relationships with parents. In *Lessons from high-performing Hispanic schools*, edited by P. Reyes, J. D. Scribner, and A. P. Scribner, 36–60. New York: Teachers College Press.

Sebring, P. B., and A. S. Bryk. 2000. School leadership and the bottom line in Chicago. *Phi Delta Kappan* 81, no. 6:440–43.

Senge, P. M. 1990. *The fifth discipline: The art and practice of the learning organization*. New York: Currency Doubleday.

Senge, P. M., A. Kleiner, C. Roberts, R. B. Ross, and B. J. Smith. 1994. *The fifth discipline fieldbook*. New York: Currency Doubleday.

Sergiovanni, T. 1984. Leadership as cultural expression. In *Leadership and organizational culture*, edited by T. Sergiovanni and J. Corbally, 121–30. Chicago: University of Illinois Press.

———. 1991. *The principalship*. Boston: Allyn and Bacon.

Sherman, A. 1994. *Wasting America's future*. Boston: Beacon Press.

Shields, C. M. 2003. *Good intentions are not enough: Transformative leadership for communities of difference*. Lanham, Md.: Scarecrow Press.

Siegel, J. 2002. The community scholar. *Harvard Magazine* (January–February): 50–54.

Singham, M. 2003. The achievement gap: Myths and realities. *Phi Delta Kappan* 84, no. 8:586–91.

Stout, L. 1996. *Bridging the class divide*. Boston: Beacon Press.

Tremmel, R. 1993. Zen and the art of reflection practice in teacher education. *Harvard Educational Review* 63, no. 4:434–58.

U.S. Census Bureau. 2001. At www.census.gov. October 7, 2002.

Valencia, R. R., ed. 1997. *The evolution of deficit thinking: Educational thought and practice*. Washington, D.C.: Falmer Press.

Valencia, R. R., and D. G. Solorzano. 1997. Contemporary deficit thinking. In *The evolution of deficit thinking: Educational thought and practice*, edited by R. R. Valencia, 160–210. Washington, D.C.: Falmer Press.

Valverde, L. A., and K. P. Scribner. 2001. Latino students: Organizing schools for greater achievement. *NASSP Bulletin* 85, no. 624:22–31.

Villani, C. J., and C. C. Ward. 2001. *Violence and non-violence in the schools: A manual for administration*. New York: Mellen Press.

Wagstaff, L., and L. Fusarelli. 1995. *The racial minority paradox: New leadership for learning in communities of diversity*. Paper presented at the annual meeting of the University Council for Educational Administration, Salt Lake City, Utah.

———. 1999. Establishing collaborative governance and leadership. In *Lessons from high-performing Hispanic schools*, edited by P. Reyes, J. D. Scribner, and A. P. Scribner, 19–35. New York: Teachers College Press.

Weinberg, L. 2001. Real welfare reform still needed for U.S. families. *Stamford Advocate*, August 20.

Werner, E. E. 1995. Resilience in development. *Current Directions in Psychological Science* 4:81–85.

Wexler, P. 1992. *Becoming somebody: Toward a social psychology of school.* London: Falmer Press.

Wheatley, M. J. 2002. *Turning to one another: Simple conversations to restore hope to the future.* San Francisco, Calif.: Berrett-Koehler Publishers.

Wilson, W. J. 1996. *When work disappears: The world of the new urban poor.* New York: Vintage Books.

Index

About the Authors

Linda L. Lyman is a professor in the Department of Educational Administration and Foundations at Illinois State University. She has a B.A. in English from Northwestern University, an M.A.T. from Harvard University, and a Ph.D. in administration, curriculum, and instruction from the University of Nebraska at Lincoln. Dr. Lyman was a faculty member at Bradley University in Peoria, Illinois, for nine years, before joining the faculty at Illinois State University in 1999. Her previous book is titled *How Do They Know You Care? The Principal's Challenge*.

Dr. Lyman has taught at the university level since 1990. Previous positions include teaching secondary English, serving as a regional staff development consultant, and being an administrative assistant at the Nebraska Department of Education. While at Bradley University she coordinated a Center for School Leadership university/school district partnership that provided professional development for urban principals. Her research, publications, and presentations have focused on leadership, with an emphasis on issues of gender, caring, and poverty.

Christine J. Villani is an associate professor in the Department of Education and Educational Foundations at Southern Connecticut State University. She has a B.S. in speech/language pathology; an M.A. in speech/language pathology; an M.A. in psychology; a sixth-year diploma in administration and supervision; and an Ed.D. in administration, policy, and urban education from Fordham University.

Dr. Villani is a former elementary principal and elementary assistant principal. She has taught and lectured on the topics of leadership, supervision, curriculum development, educational change, and school law. Dr. Villani is the author of three earlier books and various articles on the previously named topics.

Dr. Villani is an active member of the American Educational Research Association, Education Law Association, and the Association for Supervision and Curriculum Development. She is a strong proponent for integrating courses on poverty and social justice into the various education and educational leadership programs in this country.

Made in the USA
Charleston, SC
11 January 2012